DICTIONARY OF BIOLOGY

by

PARAMESHWAR HEGDE

Gaurav Book Centre Pvt. Ltd.

4832/24, Prahlad Lane, S-207 Ansari Raod, Daryaganj, New Delhi-110002

Published by
Gaurav Book Centre Pvt. Ltd.
4832/24, Prahlad Lane, S-207 Ansari Raod, Daryaganj,
New Delhi-110002
Tel.: 011-43570976, 23278261
Email-gauravbookcentre@gmail.com

First Edition : 2013

ISBN : 978-93-80317- 29-8

Price : 325/-

Laser Typesetting by : Vinod Bhardwaj

Printed at: Vikas Computers, Delhi

PRINTED IN INDIA

Published by Gaurav Book Centre Pvt Ltd,New Delhi-110002

PREFACE

Biology is a natural science concerned with the study of life and living organisms, including their structure, function, growth, origin, evolution, distribution, and taxonomy. Biology is a vast subject containing many subdivisions, topics, and disciplines.

One of the keys to being successful in biology is being able to understand the terminology. Difficult biology words and terms can be made easy to understand by becoming familiar with common prefixes and suffixes used in biology. These affixes, derived from Latin and Greek roots, form the basis for many difficult biology words. Biology words and terms that many biology students find difficult to understand. By breaking these words down into discrete units, even the most complex terms can be understood.

The present book covers thousands of Biology words and their meanigs.I hope this book would be very useful for students ,Teachers,lecturers, andalso for common people.I would like to express my sincere thanks to the publishers for their continued interest in bringingout this edition.

Parameshwar Hegde
M.Sc.,M.A.

A

Abiotic. A+biotic. Non living. For example, an abiotic factor is a non-living part of the environment.

Abductor. (levator) A type of muscle whose function is to move a limb away from the body. Adbuctors work antagonistically with adductors.

Abiogenesis. The origin of living from nonliving matter, as by biopoiesis.

Abiotic factor. Any of the nonliving factors that make up the abiotic environment in which living organisms occur. They include edaphic factors and all the aspects of climate, geology, and atmosphere that may affect the biotic environment.

Abomasum. The fourth and final chamber of the stomach of ruminants. It fills from the omasum and empties into the small intestine. The abomasum is referred to as the 'true stomach' as it is in this chamber that protein digestion occurs, in acidic conditions.

Abscission layer. Layer at base of leaf stalk in woody dicotylendons and gymnosperms, in which the parenchyma cells become separated from one another through dissolution of the middle lamella before leaf-fall.

Absorption. Uptake of water (by osmosis) and/or solutes (e.g. by simple DIFFUSION, FACILITATED DIFFUSION, ACTIVE TRANSPORT or ENDOCYTOSIS) by cells, often those forming part of a specialized epithelium.

Absorption spectrum. The amount of light taken up by a series of pigments across a particular range of wavelengths. This is important in photosynthesis because those wavelengths of light that are absorbed by the photosynthetic pigments are the wavelengths that can provide energy for photosynthesis.

Abyssal. Inhabiting deep water, roughly below 1,000 metres.

Abzyme. Monoclonal antibody with catalytic activity.

Acanthopterygli. Spiny-rayed fish. Largest superorder of (teleost) fishes. Spiny rays in their fins consist of solid pieces of bone (and not numerous small bony pieces); are unbranched and pointed at their tips. Radial bones of each ray are sutured or fused, preventing relative lateral movement. Often have short, deep bodies, and relatively large fins, making these fish very maneuverable.

Acari. Order of ARACHNIDA including mites and ticks. External segmentation much reduced or absent. Larvae usually with three pairs of legs, nymphs and adults with four pairs. Of considerable economic and social importance as many are ectoparasites and vectors of pathogens.

Accessory bud. A bud generally situated above or on either side of main axillary bud.

Accessory nerve. Eleventh cranial nerve of tetrapod vertebrates, unusual in originating from both brainstem and spinal cord. A mixed nerve, whose major motor output is to muscles of throat, neck and viscera.

Accessory pigment. Pigment that captures light energy and transfers it to chlorophyll a, e.g. chlorophyll b, carotenoids, phyco-biliproteins.

Acetyl CoA. A two carbon energy rich residue attached to a coenzyme called Coenzyme A. Acetyl CoA feeds the two carbon residue into the Kreb's citric acid cycle.

Acid. Any substance that when added to water donates hydrogen ions to the solution. Acids maybe strong or weak. Strong acids require only a small amount of acid to donate a certain number of hydrogen ions compared to weak acids. Strong acids include hydrochloric, nitric and sulfuric acids. The principle weak acids are the organic acids such as formic, acetic and the fatty acids. See also carboxyl group, pH, base.

Acclimation. Usually reversible regulatory biochemical and/or physiological compensation enabling increased tolerance to changes in an animal's external or interal environment as studied under laboratory conditions.

Acclimatization. Naturally induced, and usually reversible, regulatory biochemical and/or physiological compensation enabling increased tolerance to changes in animal's external or internal environment.

Accommodation. Changing the focus of the eye. In man and a few other mammals occurs by changing the curvature of the lens; at rest lens is focused for distant objects and is focused for near objects by becoming more convex with contraction of the ciliary mus-cles in the CILIARY BODY. See EYE, OCULOMOTOR NERVE.

Acellular. Term sometimes applied to organisms or their parts in which no nucleus has sole charge of a specialized part of the cytoplasm, as in unicellular organisms.

Acentric (Of chromosomes) chromatids or their fragments lacking any CENTROMERES.

Acetabulum Cup-like hollow on each side of hip gridle into which head of femur fits, forming hip joint in tetrapod vertebrates.

Activation energy. The amount of energy that must be added to the reactants (starting materials) in a chemical reaction in order for the chemical reaction to go to completion. This is an important concept in biology because enzymes operate by lowering the amount of activation energy required for biologically important reactions.

Active Transport. Refers to a series of energy requiring methods used by cells to get molecules, atoms or ions into or out of the cell. The energy used by these methods is generally ATP and the cell is typically acting against the natural tendency of diffusion.

Active Site. The active site is that region of the enzyme where the chemical reaction catalyzed by the enzyme takes place. The enzyme plus the chemicals involved in the reaction are jointly called the enzyme substrate complex.

Adaptation. 1.) Any physical, chemical or behavioral product of evolution that is important for the survival of an organism in it's usual environment. 2.) A physiological change in the state of an organism in response to an environmental change and that has the effect of restoring the organism's homeostasis.

Adaptive radiation. A common biogeographical pattern seen on remote islands in which a particular group of organisms is found in a wide variety of niches including many not normally inhabited by the group. Scientists infer that this pattern comes about by the an ancestral species evolving into all these niches giving rise to new species.

Adaptive zone. The way of life or functional role of an organism as seen from an evolutionary point of view. The idea is that once an evolutionary lineage has contact with a potential adaptive zone such as night flying insect eater then that lineage can evolve into that zone if its not completely occupied.

Adenosine tri-phosphate (ATP). A nucleotide like compound containing three phosphate groups. ATP is important because it serves as the principle means of energy transfer between energy producing and energy using reactions of the cell. When ATP gives up its energy it does so by a transfer of the last phosphate group to another molecule. After the energy transfer, the remainder from the ATP is called Adenosine diphosphate or ADP.

Adhesion. The tendency of unlike substances to stick together. In biology water being polar is said to adhere to other substances such as cellulose that also have polar groups. Contrast with cohesion.

Aerobic. Literally means "with air." generally refers to cellular respiration that requires oxygen. Contrast Anaerobic.

Agonistic behavior. A class of behavior that includes both aggressive and submissive behavior.

Albumin. On of a group of simple proteins, which are usually deficient in glycine. They are water-soluble and when heated coagulate.

Albuminous cell. A vertically elogonated parenchyma cell, found in groups in the rays of the secondary phloem in gymnosperms.

Alburnum. An obsolete term for sapwood.

Alcohol. A compound consisting of a hydrocarbon skeleton with one or more hydroxyl group. Ethyl alcohol is a familiar by product of yeast fermentation.

Aldohexose. An aldose sugar with six carbon atoms.

Aldopentose. An aldose sugar with five carbon atoms.

Aldose. A sugar containing an aldehyde (CHO) or potential aldehyde group.

Aldosterone. A hormone secreted by the cortex of the adrenal glands. It is a steriod, and is important in the control of sodium and potassium in concentrations in mammals.

Aleurone grain. A madified vacuole found in the embryo and endosperm of seeds and containing mostly reserve proteins, but also phytic acid and various enzymes associated with mobilization of these reserves.

Aleurone layer. The outermost proteinrich layer of the endosperm of grass furits. (e.g. cereal grains).

Aleuroplast. A type of proteoplast in which protein is stored in the form of aleurone grains. They are common in seeds; for example, in the endosperm of castor oil.

Alga(ae). A single celled or primitively multicellular aquatic eukaryotic organism that has cellulose cell walls and carries out photosynthesis.

Allele. An alternate form of a gene, in other words a gene that provides instructions for a slightly different version of the same polypeptide as the other member of a gene pair at the same location on a chromosome. See also gene, locus, chromosome.

Aliphatic compound . An organic compound with properties similar to those of merthane, ethene, ethyne, and their derivatives.

Alkaloid. One of a group of organic compounds found in plants, that are poisonous insoluble crystalline compounds.

Allantois. One of the three embryonic membranes of reptiles, birds, and mammals.

Allele. One of the possible forms of a given gene. The alleles of a particular gene occupy the same positions on homologous chromosomes.

Allopatric speciation. Evolution of new species involving the following steps: 1) isolation of an original species into two or more isolated groups due a climatic or geological event. 2) genetic divergence between the isolated groups through time due to natural selection and other mechanisms of evolution 3) Development of pre and post zygotic species isolating mechanisms. See also sympatric speciation.

Allosteric. The ability of an enzyme or other protein to exist in two or more forms. This is important because cells can exert control of an enzyme by switching it between a form with a functional active site and a form with a non functional active site. Coenzymes typically bind to a auxiliary site on the enzyme and the binding converts the enzyme from an inactive form to an active form.

Alternation of generations. The type of life cycle found in plants and some algae in which a diploid multicellular stage produces haploid spores by meiosis. The spores germinate in a suitable habitat and develop into a haploid multicellular organism which produces male and female gametes by mitosis. The gametes fuse and the diploid stage is produced from the resulting zygote by mitosis.

Altruism(Altruistic behavior). In biology, altruism is any behavior on the part of an individual organisms that benefits the reproductive success of relatives or unrelated individuals while reducing the individuals own reproductive success.

Alveolus(i). A small sac at the end of the bronchioles in the lungs. The walls of the sac consist of simple squamous epithelium which allows gas exchange between the sac and a network of capillaries which surrounds the sac. Each lung consists in part of many thousands of such sacs.

Amacrine cell. A type of nerve cell found in the retina of the eye.

Ambient. Describing the conditions and factors that are present in the immediate environment. For example, the ambient temperature is the local temperature in a specific environment.

Ameloblast. Any of the epithelial cells that secrete

enamel during tooth formation. They die before the tooth erupts, therefore damaged enamel in a tooth cannot be replaced.

Amensalism. An association between two species that is detrimental to one of the species but has no effect on the other. A common example of amensalism is the release of chemical toxins by plants that can inhibit the growth of other plant species.

Ametabolous. Describing insect development in which there is no metamorphosis and immature stages appear very similar to the adults, except that they lack genitalia. It occurs, for example, in silverfish.

Amino. A functional group containing nitrogen and hydrogen.

Amino acid. An organic compound containing an amino group at one end, a carboxyl group at the other and one of any number of functional groups from the middle carbon. The amino acid shown is glycine, the simplest amino acid. Amino acids are the building blocks of proteins.

Ammonotelic. Describing animals that excrete nitrogenous waste in the form of ammonia. Most aquatic animals are ammonotelic.

Amniotic egg. The type of egg produced by reptiles, birds, and prototherian mammals. in which the embryo develops inside a amnion. The shell of the egg is either calcium-based or leathery.

Amplification. In genetic engineering, the process by which a small amount of DNA is repeatedly duplicated to make a large amount of DNA. This can be done by inserting the DNA into a bacterial host and letting the bacteria multiply, thus making many copies of the DNA. More commonly today amplification involves an alternating sequence of mild heating and then incubation of the separated DNA halves with nucleotide bases and DNA polymerase This process is called the polymerase chain reaction or PCR.

Analogous structures. Analogous structures are structures with similar shape and function but differ in terms of their developmental origin. The inference that scientists make is that these structures do not have a common evolutionary origin.

Anabolism. The set of chemical reactions in metabolism that involve making more complex compounds from simpler compounds. For example, using amino acids to synthesize proteins is an anabolic process.

Anaerobic. Cellular Respiration without oxygen.

Androgen. This term refers to anyone of a number of steroid hormones that promote male secondary sex characteristics. Testosterone is the most familiar of these hormones, causing such characteristics as deepening voice, facial and chest hair.

Angiosperm. Flowering plant. The term refers to the fact that flowering plant seeds are hidden in a vessel rather than exposed.

Animalia. The Kingdom Animalia consists of multicellular eukaryotes. Animals do not have cell walls and are heterotrophic. Most animals ingest their food before digestion. In addition animals undergo an embryological development including a hollow ball stage called a blastula.

Antagonistic hormones. Hormones that have opposite effects and are typically part of a control system regulating the levels of a compound in the body. Insulin and glucagon are antagonistic hormones involved in regulating blood glucose level.

Antibody. A Y shaped protein produced by effector B cells(B lymphocytes)in the immune system of the body in response to the presence of certain foreign molecules or antigens produced by invading organisms. Antibodies are an important component of the body's specific defense system. Antigens are foreign molecules which in turn activate the immune system's production of antibodies that are specific to the foreign molecule.

Anticodon. A three nucleotide base triplet on transfer RNA that is complementary to a corresponding triplet on the messenger RNA. Anticodons are important because they allow the proper transfer RNA with its amino acid to attach to the ribosome, messenger RNA complex, so that the correct sequence of amino acids is produced during protein synthesis.

Antigen. A substance, generally foreign to the body that elicits an immune response. Antigens are often proteins or polysaccharides on the surface of pathogens.

Aortic arches. Six pairs of blood vessels present in all vertebrate embryos, which link the ventral aorta leaving the heart with the dorsal aorta.

Apical dominance. The phenomenon in which the presence of a growing apical bud on a plant inhibits the growth of lateral buds. It is controlled by the interactions of plant hormones, particularly auxin and abscisic acid.

Apical meristem. The actively dividing cells constituting the growing point at the tip of the root or stem in vascular plants.

Apicomplexa. A phylum of spore-forming protoctists that are parasites of animals.

Aplansopore. A non-motile spore, characteristic of the pin molds and green algae. It is an asexual spore formed in a sporangium and is usually thick walled.

Apocarpy. An ovary made up of enfused carpels, as in the buttercup.

Apoenzyme. An enzyme who-se cofactor has been remo-ved rendering it catalytically inactive. It is the protein part of a conjugate enzyme. When combined with its prosthetic group it forms a complete enzyme.

Apogamy. In pteridophytes, the development of the sporophyte directly from a cell of the gametophyte, so fusion of gametes if bypassed.

Apomixis. A modified form of reproduction by plants in which seeds are formed without fusion of gametes.

Apoptosis. Cell death either as a pre-programmed part of development or in response to chemical signals released by certain cells of the immune system.

Apoplast. The system of cell walls extending through a plant body and along which water containing mineral salts, etc. can move passively.

Apospory. The development of the gametophyte directly from the cell of a sporophyte, thus bypassing meiosis and spore production.

Appeasement. A type of behavior performed by an animal to prevent attack by another of its species.

Appendix. A blind tube or diverticulum protruding from the cecum. In humans and other primates it is small, whereas in herbivorous mammals, such as the rabbit, it is larger and contains microorganisms.

Appetitive behaviour. The first phase of a series of actions performed by a animal after initial motivation towards a specific goal.

Apposition. The deposition of successive layers of cellulose on the inner wall of a plant cell, resulting in an increase in thickness of the wall.

Aqueous humour. The fluid that fills the space in front of the lens in a vertebrate eye.

Arboreal. Animals and creatures, living in trees.

Archea(Archaebacteria). A group of prokaryotes characterized by their ability to survive in extreme environments. Some live in hot springs while others live in environments with little air. Today the Archea are considered to be in a separate kingdom from the rest of the prokaryotes.

Ascocarp. The fruiting body of ascomycete fungi in which the asci are borne. It is formed from sterile byphae surrounding the asci. If the ascocarp is closed it is termed a cleistothecium but if there is a pore through which ascospores may be discharged it is termed a perithecium or pyrencorp. An apothecium is a cup-or disk-shaped ascocarp.

Ascogonium. The female gametangium of certain ascomycete fungi. The hyphal branches bearing ascogonia become entwined with those bearing antheridia. The contents of the antheridia pass into the ascogonia and the nuclei become paired. Pairs of nuclei later fuse and meiosis takes place to give asconspores.

Ascus. The spore-producing cell of the ascomycete fungi.

It is a saclike structure that is formed either singly or in large numbers in ascocarps. After meiosis the ascus contains four or eight haploid ascospores that are liberated through a pore at the end of the sac.

Assimilation. The process of incorporation of simple molecules of food that has been digested and absorbed into living cells of an animal and conversion into the complex molecules making up the organism.

Association. A climax plant community named according to the dominant type of species. Examples are heath associations and coniferous forest associations.

Asexual. Referring to any one of a number of common reproductive methods based on mitosis and thus producing offspring that genetically identical or clones of the parent..

Atlas. A ringlike bone in tetrapods that forms the first neck vertebra of the vertebral column, on which the skull rests. In reptiles, birds, and mammals, it articulates with the skull to allow nodding of the head ad articulates with the axis to allow rotatory movement.

Atrophy. The shrinking in size of a tissue or an organ.

Attenuation. The loss of virulence of a pathogenic microorganisms after several generations of culture in vitro. Artenuated microorganisms are commonly used in vaccines.

Atom. The smallest unit of matter that can partake of chemical reactions and that has the chemical properties of an element.

Atomic number. The number of protons in an an atom. For instance, oxygen with an atomic number of 8 has eight protons in its nucleus.

Auditory. Part of vertebrate skill, enclosing auditory organ.

Autocatylist. A chemical that enhances the production of copies of itself without getting destroyed in the process.

Autotroph. An organism that obtains its energy either from sunlight or from simple compounds. For instance trees carry out photosynthesis and thus are autotrophs.

Australasia. One of the six main zoogeographical areas, composed of Australia and islands of its continental shelf, Tasmania, New Guines, and New Zealand. Marsupial and monotreme mammals are particularly characteristic, but many other unique vertebrates and invertebrates are also found.

Autecology. The study of the interactions of an individual organisms or a sngle species with the living and nonliving components of its environment.

Autoclave. An apparatus, similar in principle to a pressure cooker, in which materials are placed to be sterilized by steam under pressure. High temperatures, well above the boiling point of water, can be achieved in autoclaves.

Autoecious. Denoting rust fungi that require only one bost species to complete the various stages of their life cycle. An example is Puccinium antirrbini found on antir ehinum.

Autograft. A type of graft involving transplantation of tissue or an organ from one part of an individual to another part of the some individual.

Autoimmunity. A diseased state in which antibodies are formed and react against a normal component of the animal's own tissues. Autoimmunity is a contributory factor of a number of diseases, such as rheumatoid arthritis and some forms of gout.

Autolysis. The self-destruaction of cells by digestive enzyme activity. It is the final stage if cell senescence resulting in complete digestion if all cell components.

Autonomic movements. Mo-vements of plants in response to internal rather than external stimuli. Examples are cytoplasmic streaming, chromosome movement during nuclear division, and growth itself.

Autophagy. The process whe-rely redundant, faulry, or ageing cell organelles are destroyed. The organelle or cell portion is surrounded by a membrane derived either from the endoplasmic reticulum or a vacuole.

Autopolyploidy. A type of polyploidy involving the multiplication of chromosome sets from only one species.

Autoradiography. A techinque whereby a thin slice of tissue containing a radioactive isotpe is placed in contact with a photographic plate. The image obtained in development shows the distribution of the isotope in the tissue.

Autosomes. Paired somatic chromosomes that play no part in sex determination.

Autotetraploid. An autopolyploid that has four times the haploid number of chromosomes.

Autotomy. Self-amputation of a trapped or damaged part of the body of certain animals, especially lizards, arthropods, and worms. The lost part is usually regenerated. A special muscular mechanism exists, such that contraction along one of the various lines of weakness results in separation at that point.

Autotrophism. A type of nutrition in which the principal source of carbon is in organic. Organic materials are synthesized from inorganic starting materials.

Auxanometer. An instrument designed to measure the increase in length of a plant part. Agrowing plant is attached by thread to the end of a lever that magnifies any growth movement. The opposite end of the lever is used to record a trace on a slowly rotating dum.

Axenic culture. A culture containing only one species of microorganism.

Axil. The angle between the upper side of a leaf or branch and the shoot bearing it. Leaf axils are the site of lateral buds.

Axis. A bone in tetrapods that forms the second and strongest neck vertebra of the vertebral column. In reptiles, birds, and mammals, it bears a process, which projects upward into the 'ring' of the atlas and acts as a pivor for rotation of the head.

Axon. The part of a neurone that conveys impulses from the cell body towards a synapse. It is an extension of the cell body and consists of an axis cylinder, surrounded in most vertebrates by a fatty sheath, outside which is a thin membrane.

Axoneme. The central '9+2' core of microtubules found in cilia and flagella of eukaryotes, consisting of nine pairs of outer microtubules surrounding two single central microtubules.

Azotobacter. A genus of free-living aerobic nitrogen-fixing bacteria found in lime-stone soils and water. The cells are plump rods or cocci, surrounded by slime. A multilayered wall may be synthesized around the cell to produce a microcyst resistant to desiccation.

B

Blymphocyte (B cell). Cells in the immune system that can antibodies. These are the only cells in the immune system that can produce antibodies.

Bacillus. A rod shaped bacterium.

Bactericidal. Used to describe a compound that has a lethal effect on bacteria. A bactericidal compound may act by interfering with a vital biochemical pathway, or by destroying the molecular structure of the cell.

Bacteriostatic. Used to describe a compound that prevents reproduction of bacteria, but does not kill them.

Bacteriophage. A virus that uses bacteria as its host.

Baleen Parallel horny plates that grow down from the sides of the upper, jaw in baleen whales. 150-400 plates may occur on each side, each roughly triangular in shape and comprised of hollow fibers, which on the inner edge separated out into a fringe. They are used to strain their food, krill, from the sea water.

Bark. The outermost tissue of the stem and roots in woody plants. If the same cork cambium functions from year to year, then the bark is smooth and consists only of tissue external to the phloem, mainly cork. If new cork cambia arise every few years then the bark includes dead phloem and cortex as well as cork, and is termed rhytidome. The texture and patterning of the bark is often characteristic of the species.

Barr Body. An inactivated X chromosome. In mammals during development one X chromosome in a lineage of cells is randomly placed in a Barr body, making females in a sense, genetic mosaics.

Base pairing. The linking together of the two helical stands of DNA by bonds between complementary bases, adenine pairing with thymine and guanine pairing with cytosine. The specific nature of base pairing enables accurate replication of the chromosomes and thus maintains the constatnt composition of the genetic material. In pairing between DNA and RNA the uracil of RNA pairs with adenine.

Base. A substance that when added to water, lowers the concentration of hydrogen ions in a solution. Bases may be either weak or strong. Strong bases include sodium and potassium hydroxide. Weak bases include urea and other nitrogen containing organic compounds. See acid, pH

Base substitution. A kind of mutation in which a nucleotide with one nitrogen base, Thymine for instance, replaces another. Often this leads to a different amino acid in translation of a codon.

Basidiocarp. The fruiting body of the basidiomycete fungi, excepting the rusts and smuts. The basidiocarp is the above-ground portion of the fungus that is commonly referred to as the toadstool. It may be of a fleshy, corky, or spongy nature. The basidio-carp contains the basidial hyphae that, after meiosis, give rise to the basidiospores.

Basidium. The cell of the basidiomycete fungs that produces the haploid basidiospores. The basidial develop in the basidiocarp from hyphal tips in the hymeium and may be club-shaped or cylindrical. A basidium usually produces four basidiospores, which develop externally on short stalks called sterigmata.

Basifixed. Stamens in which the anther lobes are attached at their base to the filament, and are not capable of independent movement.

Basipetal. Developing from the apexdownwards so that the youngest structures are furthest from the apex. Basipetal differentiation is seen in the formation of proto and metaxylem in the stem. The term may also be applied to the movement of substances towards the base, for example the movement of auxin in shoot tissues.

Basophil. A white blood cell that releases histamine and other chemical messengers as part of the in flammatory response. The name comes from the fact that these cells take up certain alkaline (basic) stains.

Behavior. An organism's coordinated response to internal and external stimuli. Sometimes behavior is defined so as to refer only to animals but this is now often considered to be excessively narrow. Even bacteria can show coordinated responses to stimuli.

Benthic. Describing organisms that live on or in the sea bed. Benthic epifauna live upon the seafloor or upon bottom objects and benthic infauna live within the surface sediments.

Benzene. A colorless liquid hydrocarbon with a characteristic odor. Benzene is a highly toxic compound and continued inhalation of the vapor is harmful. It was originally isolated from coal tar and for many years this was the principal source of the compound.

Bergmann's rule. States that in geographically variable species of ENDDTHERMIC animals, body size tends to be larger in cooler regions of a speciesange, selection at low temperature allegedly favouring individuals with small surface area/body mass ratios on account of their reduced heat loss.

Berry. Many-seeded succulent fruit, in which the wall consists of an outer skin enclosing a thick fleshy mesocarp and inner membranous endocarp, as in gooseberry, currant, tomato.

Beta blocker. Substance, such as the drug propranolol, selectively blocking BETA RECEPTORS. Clinical use is to slow heart rate and lower blood pressure so that there is less hydraulic stress and consequent wear and tear on the walls of the arteries. They reduce the incidence of strokes and heart attacks.

Beta-globulins. A class of vertebrate plasma proteins including certain lipoproteins, TRANSFERRIN and plasminogen.

Beta-oxidation. An iterative series of reactions shortening a fatty acid chain by two carbon atoms at a time. Has been shown to occur in PEROXISOMES.

Bicollateral bundle. The arrangement of tissues in the vascular bundles in which the phloem is situated on both sides of the xylem. This is thought to aid transport of nutrients in plants with long trailing stems, such as the marrow.

Bilateral Symmetry. A body plan in which both haves of the body are mirror images of each other such that this can only be done in one way. We are bilaterally symmetric.

Bile. A substance produced by the liver and that contains cholesterol lecithin(a phospholipid) and various salts. The function of bile(aside from looking really gross) is to emulsify fats so that the fats can be more easily digested. Remember, bile is produced by the **liver** and stored by the **gall bladder.**

Bile duct. A duct in vertebrates that transports bile from the liver to the duodenum.

Binary fission. Non mitotic division of a bacterial cell and its DNA into two identical daughter cells.

Biogeography. The study of the distribution of plants, animals and other organisms on the earth and the development of theories to explain these distributions.

Bioluminescence. The conversion of chemical energy in a "cold" light that happens in certain organisms. Aside from the familiar "fireflies", this process happens in many other insects, bacteria, fungi, protista as well as various animals including deep sea fish. The significance of bioluminescence is not known in many of these cases.

Biome. A large scale terrestrial ecosystem characterized by certain forms of vegetation adapted to the amounts of light, moisture and the temperature found in a particular broad region.

Biosphere. The regions on, the surface, below the surface and up into the atmosphere where life is found. Sometimes considered to be the global ecosystem or ecosphere.

Biosynthetic pathway. A series, often complex, of chemical reactions which lead to the production of a chemical from simpler reactants that occurs within cells. Examples of biosynthetic pathways would be protein synthesis and the synthesis of glucose in photosynthesis.

Biotic potential. The maximum rate of increase of a population assuming ideal conditions.

Bladderworm. A larval stage of some tapeworms, consisting of a fluid-filled saccontaining an inverted scolex. It develops in the muscle of the secondary host and matures into an adult worm in a primary host that eats this infected tissue.

Blastocoel. The internal fluid-filled cavity of a blastula, which first appears during cleavage of the egg. The cavity seen in sections of chick and fish eggs, between the blastoderm and yolk, is not a blastocoel but an artefact of histological processing.

Blastocyst. A mammalian egg in the later stages of cleavage, before implantation. It consists of a hollow fluid-filled ball of cells and the inner cell mass, from which the embryo develops.

Blastoderm. The cellular mass that results from cleavage of the cytoplasm of very yolky eggs, such as those of birds, sharks, and cephalopods. The term is also used for the cellular coat of cleaved insect eggs.

Blastomere. One of the cleavage products of an animal zygote. The zygote usually divides into two, then four, then eight blastomeres, and so on until the normal nuclear/cytiplasmic ratio of the embryo's cells is achieved.

Blastopore. The opening in a gastrula between the archenteron and the outside, through which invagination occurs at gastrulation. In amniotes it is represented by the primitive streak. The dorsal lip of the amphibian gastrula is the primary organizer of the axial structure of the embryo and corresponds to Hensen's node in a chick or mammal; the future notochord is invaginated over this lip.

Blastula. The stage in an animal embryo following cleavage. It is a hollow fluidfilled ball of cells.

Blastoderm. They layer of cells that surrounds the central cavity of a blastula. In yolky eggs, such as those of insects, the blastoderm forms a layer covering the yolk.

Blind spot. The portion of the retina at which blood vessels and nerve fibres enter the optic nerve. There are no rods or cones in this area, so on visual image can be transmitted from it.

Blood-brain barrier. The mechamism that controls the passage of substances from the blood to the cerebrospinal fluid bathing the brain and spinal cord. It takes the form of a semipermeable lipid membrane permitting the passage of solutions but excluding particles and large molecules. This barrier provides the central nervous system with a constant environment, while not interfering with the transport of essential meta-bolites.

Blood cell. Any of the cells that are normally found in the blood plasma. These include red cells and white cells.

Blood serum. Blood plasma from which the fibrin and clotting factors have been removed by centrifugation or vigorous stirring, so that it cannot clot. Serum containing a specific antibody or antitoxin may be used in the treatment or prevention of certain infections. Such serum is generally derived from a nonhuman mammal.

Bohr effect. The phenomenon whereby the affinity of the respiratory pigment of the blood for oxygen is reduced as the level of carbon dioxide is increased. This facilitates gaseous exchange, because more oxygen is released in the tissues where the amount of carbon dioxide is rising due to metabolic activity. At the same time, more oxygen is taken up at the lungs or gills where the amount of carbon dioxide is low.

Botany. The scientific study of plants.

Bottleneck effect. A loss of genetic variability in a population brought about by a population crash(the bottle neck). When the population increases again, much of the population's genetic variation has been lost by passage through the bottle neck. This is important because the new population, even though it may seem healthy, is endangered because it has lost critical genetic variation to help it evolve when environmental conditions change.

Bowman's capsule. In the kidney, this is the cup shaped structure at the beginning of the nephron that receives water, urea and other substances from the blood.

Bract. A modified leaf with a flower or inflorescence in its axil. Bracts are often brightly coloured and may be mistaken for the petals of a flower. For example the showy 'flowers' of poinsettia and Bougainvillea are composed of bracts; the true flowers are comparatively inconspicuous.

Bracteole. A reduced leaf that arises from the stalk of an individual flower.

Bradycardia. A decrease in heart rate.

Bradymetabolism. Metabolism that is sustained at a relatively low rate. It is characteristic of 'cold blooded' animals and generally excludes any specific heat-generating mechanism.

Breed. A domesticated variety of an animal or, rarely, a cultivated variety of plant. Cultivated plants are usually called varieties or cultivars. Examples of animal breeds are Friesian cattle and Shetland sheepdogs.

Bronchiole. A fine respiratory tube in the lungs of reptiles, birds, and mammals. It is formed by the subdivision of a bronchus and in reptiles and mammals it terminates in a number of alveoli.

Bronchiole. A "small bronchus". The smallest of a series of finer and finer branchings from the bronchi. The bronchioles terminate in the alveoli where gas exchange between the lungs takes place.

Bronchus. In the lung, the bronchi are the primary, secondary and tertiary branchings from the trachea.

Brush border. A region of surface epithelium that possesses densely packed microvilli rather like the bristles of a brush. This greatly increases the surface area of the epithelium and facilititates the absorption of materials. Brush borders are found in the convoluted tubules of the kindly and in the lining of the small intestine.

Bryophyte. A member of the plant kingdom that lacks vascular tissue and that has a photosynthetic gametophyte from which grows the spore producing stages. Mosses and Liverworts are typical bryophytes.

Bulb. Organ of vegetative reproduction; modified shoot consisting of very much shortened stem enclosed by fleshy scale-like leaves or leaf-leaves.

Bulbil. Dwarf shoot occurring in place of a flower, borne either in lower part of the inflorescence or in axils of leaves and serving as an orga of vegetative reproductions.

Bulla, auditory. Overall movement of water or some other liquid induced by gravity or pressure or the interplay of both.

Buffer. In biology a buffer is a substance that helps a solution maintain a certain pH even though hydrogen ions are being added to or subtracted from the solution. They do this by either taking up the excess hydrogen ions or by releasing more as needed. Buffers are important because the cell's pH must typically be maintained within a narrow range for the enzymes to function properly.

Bundle scar. The scar from a vascular bundle remaining on a leaf scar after ABSCISSION

Bundle sheath. Layer of cells which surrounds a vascular bundle, comprising cells of PARENCHYMA, SCLERENCHYMA, or both.

Bulk flow. Movement of water or other substance which is due to pressure or density differences from one region of the solution to another.

Bursa of Fabricius. Thymus-like LYMPHOID organ found in birds, but not in mammals, developing dorsally from CLOACA. Like the mammalian THYMUS, it is a specialized site for a CELL maturation. Contains ANTIGEN PRESENTING CELLS.

Buttress root. An ADVENTITIOUS root on a stem, functioning in support; found mainly in monocotyledonous plants.

C

Calcicole. Describing plants that thrive on neutral to alkaline chalk, carboniferous, or limestone soils, such as marls.

Calcifuge. Describing plants that grow on soils containing very little calcium carbonate, sush as loams. Calcifuge plants are generally absent from chalky soils.

Calcitonin. A polypetide hormone, produced by the C-cells of the thyroid gland, that lowers the concentration of calcium in the blood. It acts by preventing calcium and phosphorus from leaving bone but not from entering it, thus antagonizing the effect of parathyroid hormone.

Callose. An insoluble carbohydrate that is laid down around the perforations in sieve plates. As the sieve tube ages the callose layers become thicker, eventually blocking the sieve element. Such blocking may be seasonal or permanent.

Callus. A mass of undifferentiated parenchyma cells formed by the cambium in response to wounding of the vascular tissue. If parenchyma is injured, then the surrounding uninjured parenchyma cells form a cork cambium that produces a layer of suberized cells sealing off the wound.

Calorimetry. The measurement of thermal changes involved in chemical or physical reactions, in either an in vitro system or an intact organism. For example, a bomb calorimeter is used to determine the calorific value of foods. This is a steel chamber in which the foodstuff is placed and ignited, in the presence of oxygen. The increase in temperature of water in a jacket surrounding the calorimeter indicates the heat produced by the oxidized food.

Calorie. A unit of energy used in biology. One calorie with a small "c" is roughly defined as the amount of heat it takes to raise one cubic centimeter of water from 14.5 degrees to 15.5 degrees centigrade. The food Calorie "C" is one thousand regular calories or one kilocalorie.

Calyptra. A layer of cells derived from the venter of the archegonium that covers the developing sporophyte. In bryophytes it ruptures as the seta elongates, being taken up as a hood over the capsule in mosses, and forming the sheath of tissue at the base of the seta in liverworths. The presence of the calyptra is necssary for the proper development of the the capsule in mosses and the embryo in ferns.

Calyptrogen. A layer of meristematic cells covering the root apical meristem in some plants that gives rise to the root cap.

Calyx. The outermost part of a flower, enclosing the other floral parts during the bud stage. It consists of leaflike sepals, which are normally green. The symbol K denotes the calyx in the floral formula. If the sepals are joined at their lateral margins a calyx is formed, the mouth of which may be extended into lobes or teeth.

Calvin-Benson cycle. Part of the dark reactions of photosynthesis where carbon is incorporated into the plant's metabolic pathway from carbon dioxide and used to make PGAL.

CAMP (Cyclic adenine monophosphate). An important secondary messenger in cells. One of its functions is to set up a series of chemical reactions in the cytoplasm of cells in response to non steroid hormones joining with the hormone receptor on the cell membrane.

Capillary. A capillary is a tiny blood vessel with walls only a single cell thick. Gas and nutrient exchange between the blood and the rest of the body take place only though the capillaries!

Carbohydrate. A carbon compound consisting of carbon hydrogen and oxygen in the molecular ratio of approximately one carbon : two hydrogens: one oxygen. Sugars and compounds built from sugars are the most commonly encountered carbohydrates.

Carbon. An element with an atomic number of 6 and an atomic mass of a bit more than 12. Carbon is important to biology because of carbon's strong tendency to form pure covalent bonds. Thus carbon atoms provide the skeletal framework of the molecules found in living things. Naturally pure carbon is found in three forms; graphite, buckminsterfullerine and its variants, and diamonds. It might be some some interest to diamond purchasers to note that diamonds eventually will decay into graphite.

Carboxyl. Refers to a functional group containing a carbon atom double bonded to an oxygen and single bonded to a hydroxyl(OH) group. Carboxyl groups are characteristic of organic acids and thus relate to the "acid" in the name amino acid.

Carcerulus. A type of capsular fruit that breaks up at maturity into one-seeded segments or nutlets. The carcerulus is typical of the Labiate family, e.g. deadnettle.

Carcinogen. A chemical that causes cancer. Tars from cigarettes, benzene and various dyes are good examples.

Cardia. The opening from the esophagus to the stomach in vertebrates, which functions as a sphincter but is not adapted anatomically.

Cardiac muscle. The muscle of the vertebrate heart. It consists of short cylindrical fibers with branching ends that connect with each other, forming a network, so that waves of contraction can travel through the muscle from the sinoatrial node.

Cardinal vein. Either of two pairs of veins found in fish that carries deoxygenated blood back to the heart.

Carnivore. A flesh-eating animal, especially a mammal of the order Carnivora. Carnivores generally have powerful jaws, teeth modified for tearing flesh and cracking bones, and well-developed claws.

Carpel. A leaf like section of a flower's female reproductive parts(Pistil) and that contains the ovules. Cut open a grapefruit. Each of the little sections is the remnant of a carpel.

Carrying capacity. In ecology, the number of individuals of a particular species that a region can sustain indefinitely. An important concept because humans may have exceeded the carrying capacity of this planet.

Caste. Individual organisms in a social organization that have specialized functions. Castes may be temporal meaning that as the organism ages it takes on different sets of tasks within its group. Castes may also be based on morphology as in ants, bes and wasps where some species have highly specialized workers.

Catabolism. The set of metabolic reactions involved in taking complex molecules and breaking them down into simple molecules. Digestion is a set of reactions that is part of catabolism. Another example is breaking glucose down into carbon dioxide and water as part of cellular respiration.

Catalyst. A substance that speeds up a chemical reaction without being destroyed by that reaction. A real important concept in biology because without organic catalysts called enzymes, life could not exist at the temperatures that it does.

Cation. A positively charged ion, formed by removal of electrons from atoms or molecules. In electrolysis, cations are attracted to the negatively charged electrode.

Cell. In biology a structure surrounded by a membrane and containing genetic material(DNA) on the inside. These structures are capable of self maintenance, self replication, metabolism, homeostasis, and response to the environment. These structures are considered by most biologist to be the basic unit of life.

Cell mediated immunity. The part of the immune system that largely involves defense of the body by responding to infected cells rather than by the production of antibodies.

Cellulose. A polysaccharide made of repeating glucose subunits characterized by relative inability to dissolve in water. Cellulose makes up the cell walls of plants and many algae and is one of the most abundant organic compounds on the planet. Wood and cotton are examples of substances consisting of cellulose.

Centriole. A cylindrical structure made from a series of 9 paired microtubules that is involved in organization of microskeletal elements in the cells of animals and some plants. The centriole found just beneath the surface of a eukaryote flagellum or cilium is called a **basal body** while the perpendicularly paired centrioles found near the nucleus during interphase of animal cells is sometimes called the **central body (centrosome)**. The centriole is encountered during discussions of mitosis and meiosis.

Cell sap. The solution that fills the vacuoles of plant cells. It contains sugars, amino acids, waste substances, and mineral salts.

Cellulolytic. Able to digest cellulose. For example, cellulolytic bacteria, in the stomach of ruminants, digest cellulose by means of the enzyme cellulase.

Cement(cementum). A thin layer of bony material that fixes teeth to the jaw. It covers the dentine of the root of a tooth, below the level of the gum, and is attached to the periodontal membrane lining the tooth socket in the jawbone.

Central Dogma. The basic belief originally held by molecular geneticists, that flow of genetic information can only occur from DNA to RNA to proteins. It is now known, however, that information contained within RNA molecules can also flow back to DNA, for example in the replication of retroviruses.

Central nervous system (CNS). The part of the nervous system that coordinates all neural unctions. In invertebrates it may comprise simply a few nerve cords and their associated ganglia. In vertebrates it consists of the brain and the spinal cord. The vertebrate CNS contains reflex arcs, which produce automatic and rapid responses to particular stimuli.

Centre. A part of the nervous system, consisting of a group of nerve cells, that coordinates a particular process. An example is the respiratory centre in the vertebrate brainstem, which controls breathing movements. The stimulation of a centre will initiate the process, while destruction of the cetre will prevent or impair it.

Centrifuge. A device in which solid or liquid particles of different densities are separated by rotating them in a tube in a horizontal circle. The denser particles tend to move along the length of the tube to a greater radius of rotation, displacing the lighter particles to the other end.

Centromere. A region on a chromosome where microtubules attach from the spindle during mitosis. Also serves as the point of attachment for the two chromatids in a duplicated chromosome.

Cephalization. The tendency among animal groups for the major sense organs, mouth, and brain to be grouped together at the front end of the body. These are usually contained in a specialized cephalic region-the head.

Cephalothorax. The fused head and thorax of many crustaceans and of arachnids, which is connected to the abdomen.

Cercaria. A tadpole-like larval stage of trematode worms that develops in the body of a mollusc. It subsequently infects a primary host, in which in matures into an adult worm.

Cerci. A pair of many-jointed appendages that are present on the last segment of the abdomen in certain insects, such as mayflies, earwigs, and cockroaches.

Cerebral hemisphere. Either of the two halves of the vertebrate cerebrum.

Chalone. A tissue-specific inhibitor of mitosis.

Chamaephyte. A plant life form in Raunkiaer's system of classification. Chamaephytes are essentially low-growing shrubs, in which the overwintering buds are borne above ground but near the surface to minimize exposure to the wind.

Channel. A pore formed by a protein molecule in a plasma membrane that aids the diffusion of certain substances into and out of the cell. These substances are usually charged ions or lipidin-soluble molecules.

Chela. The terminal segment of an arthropod appendage when this can be opposed to the segment that precedes it. The chela is often enlarged and modified to act as a pincer, as in the lobster. Any appendage possessing a chela is described as chelate.

Chelicerae. The first pair of appendages on the head of arachnids and other arthropods of the phylum Chelicerata. These appendages take the form of pincers of claws and are used for grasping or tearing food.

Chemical Bonds. An "attachment" between two or more atoms involving either a complete transfer of electrons (ionic bonds) or a sharing of electrons(covalent bonds).

Chemical control. The use of chemicals to kill pests.

Chemoreceptor. A cell either on the surface of an animal or inside the animal that senses the presence or change in the concentration of certain molecules and relays that information to the the central nervous system. The human nose contains a sophisticated system of chemoreceptors..... abeit not a very sensitive one.

Chemosynthetic autotroph (Chemoautotroph). An organism that obtains its energy from simple inorganic compounds such as sulfur compounds or nitrates.

Chitin. A specialized polysaccharide containing nitrogen that occurs in the exoskeleton of insects and other arthropods. Chitin also makes up a large part of the cell walls in many fungi.

Chlorophyll. Any of several green pigments, found in plants and most other photosynthetic autotrophs, the pigments all having a characteristic set of rings containing carbon and nitrogen along with a magnesium atom. Chlorophylls are important pigments in photosynthesis.

Chloroplast. A bacteria like green organelle in the cells of plants as well as in many protists. This organelle is the site of photosynthesis and gets its name from the presence of the green pigments, the chlorophylls.

CHNOPS. An acronym for the most abundant elements in living things: Carbon, hydrogen, nitrogen, oxygen, phosphorus and sulfur.

Chromatid. A single molecule of DNA and associated proteins found as part of a duplicated (replicated) chromosome.

Chromosome. A chromosome is one or two large DNA molecules and associated proteins that behave as a single unit in the cell.

Chyme. Partially digested food as it leaves the vertebrate stomach.

Cilium. A short hair like structure on the surface of many cells. Cilia are typically much shorter than the length of the cells they are part of, and have a return and a power stroke involving the whole length of the structure. The plural of cilium is **cilia**.

Cigarette smoking. For health-related aspects.

Ciliary feeding. Variety of feeding merchanism by which many softbodied aquatic invertebrates draw minute water-borne food particles through e.g. gills or the pharyngeal region of the gut, when the particles are frequently trapped in mucus and moved either towards the gut or further along it (by peristalsis).

Ciliated epithelium. Layer of columnar cells with apices covered in cilia whose coordinated beating enables CILIARY FEEDING, movement of mucus in the respiratory tract, etc.

Ciliophora. Protozoan Subphylum containing the solitary Class CILIATA.

Circinate vernation. Coiled arrangement of leaves and leaflets in the bud; gradually uncoils as leaf develops further, as in ferns.

Circulatory system. System of vessels and/or spaces through which blood and/or lymph flows in an animal.

Cirripedia. Barnacles and their relatives. Subclass of CRUSTACEA. Typically marine, sessile and hermaphrodite. Unlike most of the Class in appearance, with a carapace comprising calcareous plates enclosing the trunk region. Usually a cypris larva, which becomes attached to the substratum by its 'head', remaining fixed throughout its adult life and filter-feeding using BIRAMOUS APPENDAGES on its thorax. Several parasitic forms occur.

Cisternae. Flattened sac-like vesicles of ENDOPLASMIC RETICULUM AND GOLGI APPARATUS intimately involved in transport of materials via vesicles which either bud from or fuse with their membranous surfaces.

Cladistic. Describing the evolutionary pathways of taxonomic groups, particularly the relationships between organisms due to recent common ancestry.

Cladode. A modified internode of the stem that functions as a leaf, being flattened and highly photosynthetic. It is a xerophytic adaption and is seen in butcher's broom and asparagus.

Cladogenesis. The branching of an evolutionary line two or more separate lineages.

Class. A taxonomic rank that is subordinate to a phylum and superior to an order. Classes may be divided into subclasses.

Clavicle. One of a pair of bones that lie anteriorly, on each side of the base of the neck, in some vertebrates; they form the collar bones in humans. In humans and many other mammals they form the ventral side of the pectoral girdle, extending from the scapulae to the sternum, and serve as props for the shoulders. They are membrane bones.

Clearing. In the preparation of permanent microscope slides, the stage between dehydration and embedding, the purpose of which is to remove the dehydrating agent and replace it by a substance that is miscible with the embeddig substances. Clearing also renders the tissues transparent. Clearing agents include benzene and xylene.

Cleidoic egg. An egg with a tough shell, which permits gaseous exchange but restricts water loss (although it may take up water). Characteristic of reptiles, birds, and insects, it usually has a large food store (yolk and, in birds, albumen).

Cleistogamy. The production of closed flowers. It is a method of ensuring self polination and occurs towards the end of the flowering season in ceratin plants when no seed has been set vy the cross-pollinating flowers.

Cleavage. A chemical reaction in which a large molecule is broken apart into two or more subunits. Usually in biological systems the net effect is to add water to the molecules, hence this type of cleavage is called **hydrolysis**.

Climax. The final or stable community in a succession of natural plant communities in one area under a particular set of conditions. Oakwood is the natural climax vegetation in much of Britian, but on chalk it is beechwood. A climax is self perpetuating and in equilibrium with the physical and biotic environment. It can be held at any stage by biotic factors, such as grazing on chalk downland.

Cline. A graded series of characters exhibited by a species or other related group of organisms, usually along a line of environmental ir geographical transition. The populations at each end of the cline may be substantially different from each other.

Clinostat. An apparatus used in tropism experiments to remove the unidirectional lifluence of a stimulus on a plant organ. Typically it consists of a clockwork or electric motor with an arm to which a chamber containing growing seedings can be attached. Slow rotation of the arm results in all parts of seedings receiving an identical stimulus.

Clone. A group of cells or organisms that are derived by mitosis from another organism. Clones happen naturally as part of asexual reproduction in many organisms, but clones have become of some interest in biotechnology.

Clonal selection. In the immune system the process by which only those cells able to produce an appropriate antibody to an antigen or otherwise respond in an appropriate manner to the antigen are stimulated to multiply.

Clisere. A succession of climax communities in a given area, each giving way to the next as a result of climatic changes.

Clitoris. A small erectile rod of tissue in female mammals that lies anterior to the vagina and urethra. It is homologous with the male penis.

Cloaca. In most vertebrates, the single chamber into which the alimentary canal, kidney ducts, and genital ducts discharge their contents. In placental mammals there are two separate openings for feces, urine, and gametes.

Clotting factors. A group of substances that are activated when blood leaves the circulatory system, usually by injury, and cause blood clotting. They include 14 or so proteins, calcium ions, and platelets.

Codominance. A mode of inheritance in which the heterozygote has a phenotype that is different the phenotypes of either homozygotes. For instance for human blood type, if one homozygote is Type A, the other Type B, then the heterozygote will be Type AB. Codominance arises if both genes in the gene pair express a product.

Codon. A triplet of three nucleotide bases in messenger RNA that relate to an amino acid in the translation part of protein synthesis or an instruction to stop translation.

Coenzyme. A Non protein organic molecule that functions along with an enzyme to either activate or deactivate the enzyme. Organic **cofactors**.

Coevolution. The idea that in a biological community, the adaptations that arise in different species are at least in part in response to selective pressures put on the species by each other. For example flowers and their pollinators coevolve with respect to each other.

Cofactor. A chemical that works cooperatively with an enzyme to enhance the enzyme's catalytic ability. Cofactors maybe metallic ions or small organic molecules.

Cohesive. The tendency of a substance to stick to itself or stick together. Water molecules tend to stick together, a property that is important for living things.

Commensalism. A type of symbiosis in which one species benefits but the other species is neither harmed or benefited by the relationship. Certain mites that live in the skin of our faces are a good example.

Community. In ecology..all the populations of all the species living a particular area.

Compound. A compound is a molecule consisting of at least two different elements. For example the molecule carbon dioxide is a compound but oxygen gas is also a molecule but not a compound.

Concentration gradient. A change in the number of molecules of a particular substance per unit volume between two points. The steeper the concentration gradient the greater the difference in concentration between the two points.

Condensation reaction. A type of chemical reaction in which two or more simple molecules are joined together to make a more complex molecule. In biology the most common type of condensation reaction takes place by effectively removing a water from two molecules being joined. This type of condensation reaction is called a **dehydration synthesis**.

Conditioning. A change in the behavior of an animal based its ability to associate an environmental signal with some sort of positive or negative outcome. In **classical conditioning** the animal learns to associate an outcome with an environmental signal that normally is not associated with the outcome. For example, Pavlov's dogs learned to salivate upon hearing a bell that was rung whenever food was presented. In **operant conditioning** the organism provides its behaviors based on the results it obtains while manipulating its environment. Thus, caged pigeons can learn that pecking a certain red button will lead to the release of a food pellet or other reward.

Conjugation. A process by which genetic material is exchanged between two cells through a bridge of cytoplasm that connects the cells. This happens in bacteria and in many protists.

Consumer. A an organism that feeds on plants or other autotrophs or feeds on other consumers (e.g. a predator)

Control group. In an experiment, a group of subjects that have all variables the same as those found in an experimental group except for just the variables being investigated in the experiment.

Cranium (brain case). The part of the vertebrate skull that encloses and projects the brain. It is formed by the fusion of several flattened bones, which have immovable joints between them.

Crenation. The shrinkage of cells that occurs when the surrounding solution is hypertonic to the cellular cytoplasm. Water leaves the cells by osmosis, which causes the plasma membrane to wrinkle and the cellular contents to condense.

Cretinism. The condition that results from inadequate secretion of thyroid hormones during fetal life or early infancy. The brain and skeleton fail to develop properly, resulting in mental retardation and dwarfism.

Cryobiology. The study of the effects of very low temperatures on organisms, tissues, and cells. The ability of some animal tissues to remain viable in a frozen state enables them to be preserved by freezing for future use as grafts.

Cultivar. A plant that has been developed and maintained by cultivation as a result of agricultural or horticultural practies. The term is derived from cultivated variety.

Culture medium. A nutrient material, either solid or liquid, used to support the growth and reproduction of microorganisms or to maintain tissue or organ cultures.

Cutting. A part of a plant, such as a bud, leaf, or a portion of a root or shoot, that, when detached from the plant and inserted in soil, can take root and give rise to a new daughter plant. Talking or strikling cuttings is a horticultural method for propagating plants.

Cypsela. A dry single-seeded fruit that does not split open during seed despersal and is formed from a double ovary in which only one ovule develops into a seed. It is similar to an achene and characteristic of members of the family Compositae. Such as the dandelion.

Cytidine. A nucleoside comprising one cytosine molecule linked to a dribose sugar molecule. The derived nucleotides, cytudune mono, di-, and triphosphate, participate in various biochemical reactions , notably in phospholipid synthesis.

Cytokinesis. Cytokinesis or division of the cytoplasm is the distribution of the cytoplasm into two or more daughter cells that typically happens as part of cell reproduction. Note that cytokinesis is not part of either mitosis or meiosis proper.

Cytolysis. The breakdown of cells, usually as a result of destruction or dissolution of their outer membranes.

Cytoplasm. The region of the cell that is between the nucleus and the cell membrane. In prokaryotes the region of the cell outside of the region where the DNA is located.

Cytosine. A pyrimidine derivative. It is one of the principal component bases of nucleotides and the nucleic acids DNA and RNA.

Cytostome. A mouthlike structure of certain protists, through which pariculate food is ingested. The cytostome is typically located at the base of an indentation in the cell.

D

Daphnia. A genus of crustaceans belonging to the class Branchi-opoda and order Cladocera. Daphnia species have a protruding head with a pair of highly branched antennae for swimming and a single median compound eye. The five pairs of thoracic appendages form an efficient filter-feeding mechanism. Reproduction can take place without mating, i.e. by parthenogenesis. Some species exhibit cyclomorphosis.

Dark adaptation. The changes that need to take place in the eye when an animal moves from a brightly lit environment to a relatively dark one to enable objects to be seen clearly. On moving to a darker environment, the pupils dilate and rhodopsin the pigment in the rod cells that is broken down in bright light is regenerated from its constituents.

Day-neutral plant. A plant in which flowering can occur irrespectie of the day length. Examples are cucumber and maize.

Deamidation. A form of POST-TRANSLATIONAL MODIFICATION of proteins at asparaginyl and glutaminyl residues, resulting in negative charges at the site of modification, which may lead to changes in the tertiary strcture of the protein.

Deamination. Removal of an amino group, frequently from an AMINO ACID, by transaminase ENZYMES. In mammals occurs chiefly in the liver, where the amino group is used in production of UREA. The process is important in GLUCONEOGENSES, where resulting carbon skeleton yields free glucose.

Decidua. Thickened and highly vascularized mucus membrane lining the uterus in many mammals during pregnancy. Some or all of the decidua comes away with the PLACENTA at birth.

Deciduous. Shedding leaves at a certain season, e.g. autumn.

Dedicuous teeth. First of the two sets of teeth which most mammals have ; similar to second set which replaces it, but having grinding teeth corresponding only to the PREMOLARS, not to the MOLARS, of the PERMANENT SET.

Decussation. Crossing of nerve tracts from one side of the brain to the other. Some fibres of the optic nerves and corticospinal tracts of vertebrates cross over in this way, so that parts of the visual field from each retina are transmitted to contralateral optic tecta; each side of the body is served by its contralateral cerebral hemisphere.

Decomposer. An organism that obtains its energy from breaking down dead organic matter. A decomposer is often called a **saprobe**. Many fungi and bacteria are good examples.

Deductive Reasoning. Reasoning from a general concept or theory to a specific prediction. For example, knowing the general laws of gravity, and having mathematical equations for them, allows us to deduce or make specific predictions about the path of a satellite.

Deflciency disease. Disease due to lack of some essential nutrient, in particular a VITAMIN, trace element or essential AMINO ACID.

Degeneration. Reduction or loss of whole or part of an organ during the course of evolution, with the reslt that it becomes VESTIGIAL. In the context of cells it usually implies their disorganization and death.

Dehiscent. (Of fruits) opening to liberate the seeds; e.g. pea, violet, poppy.

Deletion. Type of chromosomal MUTATION in which a section of chromosome is lost, usually during MITOSIS or MEIOSIS. Unlike some mutations, deletions are not usually reversible or correctable by a SUPRESSOR MUTATION.

Deme. A local freely interbreeding group of organisms; a subpopulation.

Dentary. One of the tooth-bearing MEMBRANE BONES of the vertebrate lower jaw, and the only such bone in lower jaws of mammals, one on each side.

Dentine. Main constituent of teeth, lying between enamel and pulp cavity. Secreted by ODONTOBLASTS (hence mesodermal in origin), and similar in composition to BONE, but containing up to 70% inorganic material. Ivory is dentine.

Dendrite. The branched part of the neuron involved in receiving chemical signals from other neurons or information from the environment.

Dermal bone (membrane bone). Vertebrate bone developing directly from mesenchyme rather than from preexisting cartilage. Largely restricted in tetrapods to bones of CRANIUM, JAWS and PECTORAL, GIRDLE.

Dermal tissue. One of the three main tissue types in plants. This tissue occurs as a single layer of cells on the outer surfaces of leaves and stems where it is called epidermal tissue. Another type of dermal tissue, endodermis, separates the vascular bundle of the root from the surrounding tissues and helps to regulate what materials may enter the vascular system of the plant.

Detritovore. An organism that ingests dead organic matter (detritus) and digests this material internally. Many small animals such as sow bugs, millipedes and worms are detritovores.

Diakinesis. The period at the end of the first prophase of meiosis whe the separation of homologous chromosomes is alsmost complete and crossing over has occured.

Diamond. One of the three natural forms of carbon. The others are graphite and buckminster-fullerine.

Diaphragm. The muscular membrane that divides the thorax from the abdomen in mammals. It plays an essential role in breathing, being depressed during inspiration and raised during expiration.

Diaphysis. The shaft of a mammalian limb bone, which in immature animals is separated from the ends of the bone by cartilage.

Diastema. The gap that separates the biting teeth from the grinding teeth in herbivores. It creates a space in which food can be held in readiness for the grinding action of the teeth. This space is filled by large canine teeth in carnivores.

Diastole. The period during the cardiac cycle when the ventricles are relaxed. When measuring blood pressure if your blood pressure is 120/70, the "70" refers to your diastolic blood pressure.

Dibiontic. Describing a life cycle in which there is alternation of generations.

Dichogamy. The condition in which the male and female reproductive organs of a flower mature at different times, thereby ensuring that self fertilization does not occur.

Differentiation. In development, refers to the increased and largely irreversible specialization of cells as the or ganism develops. Recent research into cloning shows that differentiation can be reversed artificially.

Diffusion. A process by which a substance moves from a region of high concentration to a region of low concentration solely due to the thermal energy possessed by the molecules.

Digestion. The breaking down of complex food stuffs into simpler compounds by means of cleavage reactions.

Digestive system. The system of organs that are involved in the process of digestion. The digestive system of mammals is divided into the gastrontestinal tract and accessory structures, such as teeth, tongue, liver, pancreas, and gall bladder.

Digit. A finger or toe. In the basic limb structure of terrestrial vertebrates there are five digits. This number is retained in humans and other primates, but in some other species the number of digits is reduced. Frogs, for example, have four fingers and five toes, and in ungulate mammals, the digits are reduced and their tips are enclosed in horn, forming hooves.

Digitigrade. Describing the gait of most fast-running animals, such as dogs and cats, in which only the toes are on the ground and the rest of the foot is raised off the ground.

Dihybrid cross. A mating involving pure breeding individuals with respect to alternate forms of each of two characteristics. The offspring from this mating are then mated with each other to examine the mode of inheritance of the two characteristics.

Diploblastic. Describing an animal with a body wall composed only of two layers, ectoderm and endoderm, sometimes with a noncellular mesoglea between them. Coelenterates are diploblastic.

Diploid. Having chromosomes in pairs of similar chromosomes called homologous chromosomes.

Diplotene. The period in the first prophase of meiosis when paired homologous chromosomes begin to more apart. They remain attached at a number of points.

Disaccharide. A sugar consisting of two linked monosaccharide molecules. For example, sucrose comprises one glucose molecule and one fructose molecule bonded together.

Discicristates. An assemblage of eukaryotic protists whose members have discshaped cristae in their mitochondria and are shown to be related by molecular systematics. They include the euglenids, kinetoplastids, and amoebomastigotes, plus the acrasid cellular slime moulds.

Disease. A condition in whih the normal function of some part of the body is disturbed. A variety of microorganisms and environmental agents are capable of causing disease. The functional disturbances are often accopanied by structural changes in tissue.

Disinhibition. The tendency to exhibit displacement behaviour at a point of equilibrium in situations where there are two or more conflicting drives.

Distal. Describing the part of an organ that is farthest from the organ's point of attachment to the rest of the body. For example, hands and feet are at the distal ends of arms and legs, respectively.

Diuresis. The production of watery urine in large quantities. Diuresis causes the osmotic pressure of the blood to rise and is counteracted by the antidiuretic hormone.

Diverticulum. A saclike or tubular outgrowth from a tubular or hollow internal organ. Diverticula may occur as normal structures or abnormally, from a weakened area of the organ.

Division. A category used traditionally in the classification of plants that cosists of one or several similar classes. An example is the Spermatophyta. In modern classification systems the phylum has replaced the division.

DNA. DNA or Deoxyribonucleic acid is a a double stranded nucleic acid. Each strand is mad up of many units each made from phosphate, 5 carbon sugar and one of four nitrogen containing carbon bases. The function of DNA is to serve as genetic material in organisms and in some viruses.

DNA chips. Oligonucleotide arrays on a microchip platform, capable of testing for genetic disorders and ANTISENSE applications. Technique combines lightdirected synthesis and conventional oligonucleotide chemistry with DNA hybridization.

DNA gyrase. A bacterial DNA TOPOISOMERASE, adding supercoils to DNA.

DNase (deoxyribonuclease). Any enzyme that hydrolyzes the phosphodiester bonds of DNA. DNases are classified into two groups, according to their site of action in the DNA molecule.

DNA polymerase. A complex enzyme involved in the replication of DNA.

Dominant. In genetics an allele that completely masks the expression of another allele at the same locus on a homologous chromosome is said to be dominant over the second one.

Donor. A person or animal that donates blood, tissues, or organs for use by another person or animal.

Dopamine. A catecholamine precursor of epinephrine and norepinephrine. In mammals it is found in highest concentration in the corpus striatum of the brain, where it functions as an inhibitory neurotransmitter. High levels of dopamine are associated with Parkinson's disease in humans.

Dorsal aorta. In mammals, the descending portion of the aorta, which carries oxygenated blood to the trunk and hind limbs. In fish it is formed from the fusion of the six aortic arches. In tetrapods it arises from the systemic arch.

Dorsifixed. A stamen in which the filament is fused to the back of the anther.

Double fertilization. The fusion of one pollen nucleus with the egg to form the zygote and of the other pollen nucleus with a polar nucleus to form the triploid endosperm nucleus. The process is restricted to certain angiosperms.

Double recessive. An orgaisms containing both recessive alleles of a particular gene and thus expressing the recessive form of the gene in its phenotype. Double recessives, being of known genotype, are often used in test crosses to establish whether the organisms to which it is crossed is heterozygous or homozygous for the same gene.

Double bond. A covalent bond in which each of the two atoms in the bond are sharing two electrons. Hence the double bond involves a sharing of four electrons in all. In structural diagrams the double bond is shown as two lines connecting the atoms.

DRiPS. Defective ribsomal products: peptides produced in cells by enzymic digestion of the natural waste matter of protien synthesis, such as misfolded proteins and prematurely terminated polypeptides arising from errors in the synthetic machinery.

Drive. The motivation that results in a animal performing a particular activity. There are two types: primary drive. which arises as a direct result of tissue requirements; and secondary drive. resulting from learned behaviour.

Drone. A fertile male in a colony of social bees, especially the honeybee. The drones die after mating with the queen bee as the male reproductive organs explode within the female.

Drug. Any substance, e.g. neurotransmitters and hormones, capable on administration of altering the behaviour and/or physiology of an organism.

Drupe (pyrenocarp). A fleshy fruit that develops from either or several fused carpels and contains one or many seeds. The seeds are enclosed by the hard protective endocarp of the fruit. Thus the stone of a peach is the endocarp containing the seed. Plums, cherries, coconuts, and almonds are other examples of oneseeded drupes; holly and elder fruits are examples of many-seeded drupes.

Dry mass. The mass of a biological sample after the water content has been removed, usually by placing the sample in an oven. The dry mass is used as measure of the biomass of a asample.

Dryopithecus. A genus of extinct apes, fossils of which have been found in Europe and Asia and dated to the mid-Miocene. Fossils or Dryopithecus and of the similar genus Proconsul are often referred to as dryopithecines.

Duct. A tube or passage in an organism that is involved in the secretion or excretion of substances.

Ductus arteriosus. A channel that connects the pulmonary artery with the aorta in the mammalian fetus and therefore allows blood to bypass the inactive lungs of the fetus. Derived from the fifth aortic arch, it normally closes soon after birth.

Duplex. Describing a biological molecule comprising two cross-linked polymeric chains oriented lengthways side by side. The term isapplied particularly to the double-stranded structure of DNA.

Duplication. The doubling or repetition of part of a chromosome, which generally originates during the crossing over phase of meiosis. Occasionally this type of chromosome mutation may have beneficial effects on a population. For example, a beneficial duplication resulted in the evolution of four types of haemoglobin in humans and apes from a single form. One of these types of haemoglobin (gamma or fetal haemoglobin) has a greater affinity for oxygen and maximizes fetal uptake of oxygen from the mother's blood.

Duplicated Chromosome. A chromosome containing two identical molecules of DNA is called a duplicated chromosome as opposed to an unduplicated chromosome which is a chromosome with one molecule of DNA.

Dura mater. The outermost and toughest of the three membranes that surround the central nervous system in vertebrates. It lies adjacent to the skull ad its purpose is to protect the delicate inner meninges (the arachnoid membrane and the pia mater).

Dynein. A protein, found in many eukaryotic cells, that prossesses *ATP ase activity and binds to microtubules. Dynein is associated with the microtubules of *undulipodia; it moves along the microtubules, using energy derived from the hydrolysis of ATP, causing the undulipodium to bend. Dynein in the cytoplasm of cells causes the movement of organelles along the microtubules.

Dynorphin. A peptide produced as a neurotransmitter in various parts of the brain and spinal cord that binds to kappa opioid receptors. The dynorphins are thus classed as endogenous opioids, casuing analgesia among other effets. They are thought to play a role in depression and certain types of drug addiction.

Dystrophic. Describing a body of water, such as a lake, that contains large amounts of under-composed organic matter derived from terrestrial plants.

E

Ear. One of a pair of sense organs, located either sode of the head in vertebrates, that are concerned with hearing and balance. In mammals the ear consists of an outer ear, separated by the tympanum from the middle ear, which communicates, via the oval window and round window, with the inner ear. In fish only the inner ear is concerned solely with balance.

Ear, middle. Tympanic cavity. Cavity between eardrum and auditory capsule of tetrapod vertebrates. Derived from a gill pouch. Communicates with pharynx viaeustachian tube, and is filled with air, ensuring atmospheric pressure is maintained on both sides of the eardrum. In it lie the EAROSSICLES.

Ear, outer. That part of the tetrapod ear, absent from amphibians and some reptiles, external to the eardrum. Comprises a bony tube. In addition in mammals there is a flap of skin and cartilage at the outer opening which amplifies and focuses pressure ways upon the eardrum. Well developed in nocturnal mammals.

Ecdysterone. A steroid hormone, produced by arthropods, that induces molting and metamorphosis. It acts on DNA to initiate the synthesis of new proteins and enzymes involved in the process of molting and cuticle formation. Ecdysterone is formed from its inactive precursor, ecdysone, which is secreted by the prothoracic glands.

Ecesis. The germination and establishment of colonizing plants in an area, this being the first stage in a succession.

Echinoidea. The class of the Echiodermata that contains the sea urchins, found on the sea bed or buried in sand. The spherical, heart-shaped, or flattened body lacks arms and is covered by a rigid shell bearing movable spines used in locomotion and defense. The mouth, with a complicated jaw apparatus, is on the ventral suface.

Echolocation. A method used by some animals to locate objects. They emit highpitched sounds, often inaudible to humans, which are reflected back off the object and detected by the ear or other sensory receptor.

Ecological niche. The functional role of an organism in a community. If two species occupy the same niche then competition occurs until one has replaced the other. A similar niche may be occupied by different areas, for example the fallow deer of Africa occupies the same niche as the red deer of Eurasia. Conversely one type of organism may several different niches, such as the finches of the Galapagos Islands.

Ecology. The science which studies the interrelationships between different organisms with each other and with the non-living environment.

Ecospecies. A group of ecotypes within a species, between which crossing is possible without loss of fertility in the offspring.

Ecosystem. The sum of the living and non living components found in a particular area; Community plus non living environment.

Ecotype. A group of organisms within a species adapted genetically to the combination of environment factors in their habitat, but able to reproduce with other ecotypes belonging to the same species. Differences between ecotypes may be physiological or morphological.

Ectoderm. The germ layer of metazoans that remains on the outside of the embryo and develops into the epidermis and its derivatives and the lining of mouth and cloaca.

Ectoparasite. An organism that lives on the outside of another organism and benefits from the relationship at the expense of the host, such as the flea.

Ectotrophic mycorrhiza. An association between a basidimycete fungus and a woody plant. The fungal hyphae form an external covering around the root and also grow between the cells of the host root cortex.

Edaphic factors. Environmental conditions determined by physical, chemical and biological characteristic of the soil.

Edentata. Aberrant order of eutherian Mammalia, mainly of South American history and distribution. Includes three sloths, anteaters, armadillos and extinct glyptodonts. Only anteaters are truly toothless, the other having molars at least.

Endosymbiotic hypothesis. The idea that certain organelles in eukaryotic cells such as chloroplasts, mitochondria, were orginally free living organisms that became associated with the ancestors or eukaryotes.

Effector. The part of an organism that produces a change in response to a signal or stimulus.

Effector neuron A nerve cell, such as a motor neuron, that transmits impulses from the central nervous system to an effector in order to bring about a physiological response to changes in the environment.

Efferent. Leading away from; e.g. from the central nervous system from the gills.

Egestion. The expulsion from the body of waste food materials that have never left the gut, particularly the expulsion of undigested materials from the gut through the anus. Egestion should not be confused with excretion, in which the waste materials are produced by metabolic activity in the body's tissues.

Egg apparatus. The three haploid nuclei that are situated at the micropylar end of the embryo sac. The central nucleus is the female gamete and those to either side of it are called the synergids.

Elaioplast. Colourless plastid in which oil is stored; common is liverworths and monocotyl-endons.

Elastin. Principal fibrous protein of the yellow fibres of animal CONNECTIVE TISSUE. Numerous in lungs, walls of large arteries and in ligaments. Highly extensible and elastic.

Electron. Electrons are lightweight negatively charged particles that surround the atom in different shells (energy levels) and orbitals (volumes of space") within the same energy level or shell. The further on average the electron is from the nucleus the more energy the electron has. This is important since the transfer of energy in chemical reactions involves the transfer of electrons.

Electrophile. Electron-dificient functional group in molecules, which seeks electrons. Contrast NUCLEOPHILE.

Electron transport system (ETS). A series of proteins found in the plasma membranes of certain organelles and also in the cell membranes of many prokaryotes. These proteins carry electrons from one spot to another and as the electrons are carried the energy contained by the electrons is exploited to do work. This work is usually involved with making ATP.

Electrophoresis. A series of techniques which are used to separate proteins, nucleic acids or other biologically important compounds based on the relative distance traveled toward a positive or negative electrical charge. In gel electrophoresis a sample is placed in a gel and the various molecules in the sample allowed to migrate in an electric field. After a set amount of time a stain is applied and any patterns of banding observed. With proteins, the technique is used to separate alternate forms of proteins related to alternate forms of a gene.

Electrostatic. Refers to an attractive or repellent force involving positive and negative charges. Unlike charges attract, like charges repel. This is important in understanding how the properties of water come about and the assembly of phospholipid bilayers among other things.

Emasculation. Removal of stamens from hermaphrodite flowers before they have liberated their pollen, usually as a preliminary to artificial hybridization.

Enamel. Hard covering of exposed part of tooth; 97% inorganic material (two thirds calcium phosphate crystals, one third calcium carbonate), 3% organic.

Enation. Outgrowth produced by local hyperplasia on a leaf as a result of viral infection.

Endarch. Type of primary xylem maturation, characteristic of most stems, where the oldest xylem elements are closer to centre of axis than those formed later.

Endergonic reaction. A chemical reaction in which the products of the reaction have more energy than the starting materials.

Endocarp. Innermost layer of the carpel wall, or pericarp of fruit, in flowering plants. Frequently used to denote the 'stone' of drupes.

Endocrine. A gland that secretes its products(usually hormones) into the blood stream.

Endomembrane system. A series of inter working organelles beginning with the nuclear envelope and including the rough and smooth endoplasmic reticulum as well as the Golgi body and various vacuoles produced by these organelles. This network functions in the synthesis and modification of proteins as well as the synthesis of lipids and other compounds for the cell. In addition this network insures that these materials get to their proper place in the cell.

Endocytosis. The process by which cells take in bulk material from the outside, usually by surrounding the material and isolating it into a vacuole or vesicle which is then brought deeper into the cell.

Endosymbiotic hypothesis. This hypothesis says that certain organelles, chiefly mitochondria and plastids, evolved from free living bacteria that became symbiotic with the ancestors of modern eukaryotic cells.

End organ. Structure at peripheral end of a nerve fibre; usually either a RECEPTOR or a motor end-plate.

Endorphins. Peptide NEUROTRANSMITTERS, isolated from the PITUITARY GLAND, having morphine-like pain suppressing effects. Also implicated in memory, learning, sexual activity, depression and schizophrenia.

Endostyle. Ciliated and mucus-secreting groove or pocket in ventral wall of pharynxes of urochordates, hemichordates, cepaloch-ordates and ammocoete larvae ogf lampreys. The vertebrate thyroid is probably homologous with it.

Energy. The ability to do work. This ability may be stored (Potential energy) , for example chemical energy, or be in current use to bring about movement (Kinetic energy); for example light energy is kinetic energy.

Entropy. A measure of disorder or uncertainty of a system. The second law of thermodynamics is often stated as "entropy in a closed system tends to increase."

Enzyme. An enzyme is an organic catalyst produced by living things. As catalysts the function of enzymes is to speed up chemical reactions without being destroyed by those reactions. Most enzymes are proteins but today we recognize that certain ribonucleic acids also can serve as enzymes.

Eosin. One of a series of acidic dyes, usid in optical microscopy, that colours cytoplasm pink and cellulosered. It is frequently used as a counterstain with haematoxylin for colouring tissue smears and sections of animal tissue.

Eocytes. Archaebacterial sulphobacteria, thought by some to be the sister group of eukaryotes. Evidence rests on the inclusio of a ioamino acid sequence in their ELONGATION FACTOR and shared with those of eukaryotes but absent from EF1s of other archae-bacteria, all true bacteria and from all EF-2 sequences.

Epicalyxo. A ring of bracts below a flower that resembles a calyx. It is seen, for example, in the strawberry flower.

Epicotyl. The region of a seedling stem above the stalks of the seed leaves of an embryo-plant. It grows rapidly in seeds showing hypogeal germination and lifts the stem above the soil surface.

Epidemic. An outbreak of a disease that affects a large number of individuals within a population at the same time.

Epididymis. A long coiled tube in which spermatozoa are stored in vertebrates. In reptiles, birds, and mammals it is atached at one end to the testis and opens into the sperm duct at the other.

Epigamic. Serving to attract a mate. Epigamic characters include the bright plumage of some male birds.

Epigeal. Describing seed germination in which the seed leaves emerge from the ground and function as true leaves. Examples of epigeal germinantion are seen in sycamore and sunflower.

Epilimnion. The upper layer of water in a lake.

Epiphyte. A plant that grows upon another plant but is neither parasitic on it nor rooted in the ground. Epiphytes include many mosses and lichens and some trophical orchids.

Episome. A genetic element that can exist and replicate either independentaly of its host cell's chromosomes or as an integrated part of the chromosomes. Examples include certain bacterial plasmids.

Epistasis. A mode of genetic inheritance where a homozygous recessive gene pair prevents the expression of a gene pair at another locus.

Epithelial tissue. A flat tissue that covers the exterior of animals or lines the insides of glands and other cavities inside of the animal. Epithelial tissue is not penetrated by capillaries and lies on top of a nonliving membrane called a basement membrane.

Ergonomic. The study of the engineering aspects of the relationship between workers and their working environment.

Ergosterol. A sterol occurring in fungi, bacteria, algae, and plants. It is converted into vitamin D2 by the action of ultraiolet light.

Erythroblast. Any of the cells in the myeloid tissue of red bone marrow that develop into erythrocytes. Erythroblasts have a nucleus and are at first colourless, but fill with haemologlobin as they develop. In mammals the nucleus disappears.

Eserine(physostigmine). An alkaloid, derived from the calabar bean plant, that inhibits cholinesterase by covalently binding with it. Eserine is used to treat the eye condition glaucoma.

Essential oil. A natural oil with a distinctive scent secreted by the glands of certain aromatic plats. Terpenes are the main constituents. Essential oils are extracted from plants by steam distillation, extraction with cold neutral fats or solvents, or pressing and used in perfumes, flavourings, and medicine. Examples are citrus oils, flower oils, and oil of cloves.

Etaerio. A cluster of fruits formed from the unfused carpels of a single flower. For example, the anemone has an etaerio of achenes, larkspur an etaerio of follicles, and blackberry an etaerio of drupes.

Ethylene. A gaseous hydrocarbon with two carbon atoms and two hydrogen atoms. Ethylene is of interest as a plant hormone that is a also a gas. Ethylene is involved in fruit ripening and leaf fall in many plants.

Ethyl alcohol. CH_3OH The product of fermentation of pyruvic acid by yeast. Also the alcohol that people some people overindulge in.

Etiolation. The abnormal form of growth observed when plants of grow in darkness or severely reduced light. Such plnats characteristically have blanched leaves and shoots, excssively long shoots, and reduced leaves and root systems.

Eucarpic. Denoting a fungus in which the thallus is differentiated into vegetative and reproductive regions.

Eukarya. A domain containing all eukaryotic organisms, embracing protists, fungi, plants, and animals. In three-domain classification systems, the other two domains are Archaea and Eubacteria.

Eukaryotic. Refers to a cell that has a true nucleus in which the DNA is isolated from the rest of the cell by an envelope. Also, eukaryotic cells are characterized by the presence of membrane bound organelles such as mitochondria and chloroplasts.

Eumycota. In some earlier classifications, a division, or phylum, containing the 'true fungi', as distinct from slime moulds.

Eusocial. This term refers to organisms that live in complex highly organized groups characterized by division of labor and castes either temporal or morphological. Examples include wolves, humans, all ants many bees and wasps as well as termites.

Eury. A prefix denoting width of range. For example, euryhaline aquatic organisms can tolerate a wide range of saline conditions.

Evergreen. A plant that bears leaves throughout the year, each leaf being shed independently of the others after two or three years. The leaves of evergreens are often reduced or adapted in some way to prevent excessive water loss; examples are the needles of conifers and the leathery waxy leaves of holly.

Evocation. The ability of experimental stimuli to cause unspecialized embryonic tissue to develop into specialized tissue.

Evolution. 1. A change in the genetic make-up of a population. This change may lead to new adaptations within a species (**microevolution**) 2. The development of new species from pre-existing species (**speciation**)

Exarate. Designating pupae in which the wings and legs are free and which are therefore capable of limited movement.

Exarch. Denoting a stele in which the metaxylem develops to the inside of the protoxylem.

Exergonic. A chemical reaction in which energy is released, the products have less energy than the starting materials.

Exine (exosporium). The outermost wall of a spore of pollen grain. The patterningof the exine may be characteristic of the species and has become an important taxonomic character since the advent of the scanning electron microscope.

Exocrine gland. A gland that secretes its products to the outside of the body or into an internal cavity such as the small intestine. Exocrine glands may secrete pheromones, but not always. A familiar exocrine gland is the liver which secretes bile. Sweat glands are also exocrine glands.

Exodermis. An outermost layer of thickened or suberized cortical cells that sometimes replaces the epidermal layer in the older parts of roots if the epidermal cells have died.

Exogamy. The fustion of gametes produced by organisms that are not closely related.

Exogenous. Produced or originating outside an organism.

Exointine. The middle layer of the wall of a spore or pollen grain between the exine and intine.

Exonuclease. An enzyme that catalyzes the hydrolysis of the terminal linkages of polynucleotides such as DNA and RNA, therely removing terminal nucleotides.

Exosporic. The formation of spores outside the spore-producing organ. In the basidiomycete fungi, for example, the basidiospores are borne on the tips of the sterigmata, which are outgrowth of the basidium. Spore production in more commonly endosporic.

Experiment. A manipulation done on the natural world in order to test a hypothesis. Experiments usually involve comparing a control group with an experimental group where the two groups are as similar as possible except that the experimental group receives a treatment not given to the control group.

Exploratory behavior. The early activities of young animals during play, interactions with other individuals, and exploration, through which they learn about their immediate environment and acquire behaviour skills.

Extracellular. Occuring or situated outside a cell.

Extrorse. Denoting anthers in which dehiscence lines are to the outside of the flower, promoting cross pollination.

Exocytosis. The process by which cells send bulk material to the outside of a cell, usually by means of a vesicle which fuses with the cell membrane, releasing the vesicle's contents.

Exon. That part of the RNA transcript that will leave the nucleus of the cell for translation or for use to make tRNA.

F

Facial nerve. One of the pair of nerves that arises from the anterior hindbrain in vertebrates to supply the muscles of the face. It also carries sensory nerve fibres from taste buds and autonomic nerve fibres to saliary glands and the lacrimal gland.

Facilitated diffusion. The movement of a substance from a region of high concentration to a region of low concentration across a plasma membrane where this movement can only happen through special protein channels and which involves no use of energy by the cell.

Facilitation. The phenomenon in which passage of an impulse across a synapse renders the synpase more sensitive to successive impulses so increasing the postsynaptic response large enough to triger an impulse.

FAD. A derivative of riboflavin that is a coenzyme in electron-transfer reactions.

Fallopian tube. One of a pair of ducts in female mammals, also called oviducts, that conveys ova from the ovary to the womb with the and of muscular and ciliary action. It opens anteriorly into a ciliated funnel, which lies close to the ovary. The Fallopian tubes each represents the upper region of a Muillerian duct.

Family. A collection of similar genera. Families may be subdivided into subfamilies, tribes, and subtribes. Plant family names generally end in aceae whereas animal family names usually end in idae. Similar families are grouped into orders.

Fascia. A sheet of connective tissue. For example., the layer of adipose tissue under the human dermis and the sheets of tough connective tissue around muscles are types of fasciae.

Flavin adenine dinucleotide (FAD). FAD is fine....FAD is an electron acceptor found in the matrix of the mitochondrion. It is responsible along with **NAD+** for accepting electrons and hydrogen ions from the Kreb's citric acid cycle for transfer to the electron transport systems along the inner mitochondrial membrane.

Fat. A lipid with usually three relatively saturated fatty acids attached to a glycerol molecule. Oils are similar except that the fatty acids are unsaturated. Fats and oils together are collectively called **triglycerides** if they have three fatty acids per glycerol.

Fat body. A mass of fatty tissue forming a definite structure within the body cavity of some animals. In amphibians and reptiles, a pair of solid fat bodies are attached to the kidneys or near the rectum and act as a food store for use during hibernation and breeding. In insects the fat forms a more diffuse tissue around the gut and reproductive organs and stores protein and glyc ogen as well as fat.

Fat map. A map of the probable fates of the various regions of the blastula surface of animals with indeterminate development, usually show as colors; colors are assigned to the various tissues and structures of the formed embryo and, by imagining the developmental process reserved, these colored tissues are followed back to the blastula. The three major germ layers occupy large discrete areas of the fate maps of vertebrates. Mosaic eggs have cell lineages instead of fate maps.

Fatty acid. An organic acid consisting of a long non polar hydrocarbon chain with a carboxyl group at one end.

Feces. Solid or semisolid material, consisting of undigested food, bacteria, mucus, bile, and other secretions, that is expelled from the alimentary canal through the anus.

Fecundity. The capacity of an organism to produce offspring. Most organisms show such enormous fecundity that the size of their population would rapidly increase if all them survived. In practice most offspring do not survive.

Feedback. The regulation of a control mechanism by the output of the system involving the control mechanism. In **negative feedback**, output from the system inhibits the production of more output. In **positive feedback**, output from the system enhances the production of even more output. Feedback is an important concept in hormonal and nervous system control of the body as well as in the study of social and economic systems.

Fehling's solution. A freshly mixed solution used for testing for the presence of reducing sugars and aldehydes in solution. When boiled with equal amounts of Fehling's A (copper(II) sulfate solution) and Fehling's B (sodium potsassium tartrate and sodium hydroxide solution) reducing sugars and aldehydes produce a brick red precipitate of copper(I) oxide.

Fermentation. An anaerobic process by which alcohol, lactic acid or other organic compound is produced using the pyruvate produced by glycolysis.

Ferredoxins. A group of red-brown proteins found in green plants, man y bacteria and certain animal tissues. They contain non-heme iron in association with sulfur at the active site. They are strong reducing agents and function as electron carriers, for example in photosynthesis and nitrogen fixation. They have also been isolated from mitochondria.

Fibril. Any small fibre or threadlike structure.

Fibrin. The insoluble protein that forms at the site of an injury and is the foundation of a blood clot.

Fibrinogen. The protein dissolved in the blood plasma that, when suitably activated, is converted to insoluble fibrin fibres.

Fibrinolysis. The breakdown of the protein fibrin by the enzyme plasmin, which occurs when blood clots are removed from the circulation.

Fibroblast. A cell that secretes fibres in the intercellular substance of connective tissue. The cells are long, flat, and starshaped and lie close to collagen fibres. Fibroblasts are often grown in cell cultures.

Fibula. The smaller and outer of the two bones between the knee and the ankle in terrestrial vertebrates.

Field capacity. The amount of water that remains in a soil when excess has drained away. It is held by capillary forces of the soil pores and reflects the physical nature of the soil.

Filoplumes. Minute hairlike feathers consisting of a shaft bearing a few unattached barbs. They are found between the coconut feathers.

Filter feeding. A method of feeding in which tiny food particles are stained from the surrounding water by various mechanisms. It is used by many aquatic invertebrates, especially members of the plankton, and by some vertebrates, notably baleen whales.

Filtrate. The clear liquid obtained by filtration.

Filtration. The process of separating solid particles using a filter. In vacuum filtration, the liquid is drawn through the filter by a vacuum pump. Ultrafiltration is filtration under pressure, for example, ultrafiltration of the blood occurs in the nephrons of the vertebrate kidney.

Finger domain. A finger-shaped structure produced in a protein when a series of the constituent amino acids combines with a metal atom. Finger domains are often found repeated in trascription factors.

Fission. A type of asexual reproduction occurring in some unicellular organisms, e.g. diatoms, protozoans, a nd bacteria, in which the parent cell divides to form two or more similar daughter cells.

First law of thermodynamics. Under normal conditions energy cannot be created but only converted from one form to another.

Fitness. Fitness refers to the ability of an organism to leave copies of its genes relative to other organisms in the population. It may do so either by having descendants of its own(**Classical fitness**) or by influencing the reproductive success of relatives that share genes in common with it. The sum of the organism's classical fitness, plus the relative ability of the organism to leave copies of its genes found in relatives, is called **inclusive fitness**.

Fixed action Pattern(FAP). A sequence of stereotyped behaviors in response to a stimulus in the environment.

Flaccid. Describing plant tissue that has become soft and less rigid than normal because the cytoplasm within its cells has shrunk and contracted away from the cell walls through loss of water.

Flagellum. A long whip-like projection from the surface of cells and which propel the cell. Often a distinction is made between the eukaryotic flagellum and a prokaryotic flagellum which lacks microtubules. Eukaryotic flagella move internally while the prokaryotic flagella move because of energy transfer from the base.

Floral apex. Apical meristem that will develop into a flower or inflorescence.

Floral diagram Diagram illustrating relative positions and number of parts in each of the sets of organs comprising a flower.

Floral tube. Cup or tube formed by fusion of basal parts of sepals, petals and stamens. often in flowers possessing inferior ovaries.

Floret. One of the small flowers making up the composite inflorescence, or the spike of grasses. In the former, ray florets are often female while disc florets are often hermaphrodite.

Floridean starch. Polysaccharide storage product occuring in red algae ; somewhat similar to amylopectin.

Florigen. Hypothetical plant 'hormone', invoked to explain transmission of flowering stimulus from leaf, where it is preceived, to growing point.

Floristic equilibrium. The species composition of a flora when there is no further change generated internally or externally.

Floristics. Study of compositions of vegetation in terms of species present in a particular region. Floristics aims to account for all plants of the region, with keys, descriptions, ranges, habitats and phenology, and to offer analytical explanations of the flora's origin and geo-historical development.

Fluid mosaic model. The fluid mosaic model treats the cell membrane as a phospholipid bi-layer within which are embedded proteins with various functions. The phospholipid BI-layer can be thought of as the matrix of a mosaic and the proteins, the tiles.

Fluorescent antibody rechnique. Cells or tissues are treated with an antibody which has been labelled by combining it with a substance that fluoresces in UV light and can therefore indicate the presence and location of the antigen with which it combines.

FMN (flavin mononucleotide). A FLAVIN; derivative of riboflavin. Prosthetic group of some FLAVOPROTEINS.

Foetus(fetus). In mammals, the stage in intrauterine development subsequent to the appearance of bone cells in the cartilage, indicating the onset of OSSIFICATION. In humans, this occurs after seven weeks of gestation.

Follicle (Bot). Dry fruit derived from a single carpel which splits along a single line of dehiscence to liberate its seeds; e.g. of larkspur, columbine.

Follicular phase. Phase in mammalian OESTROUS and MENSTRUAL CYCLES, in which Graafian follicles grow and the uterine lining proliferates due to increasing oestrogen secretion.

Follistatins. Family of glycosylated proteins which modulate pitutary FSH release and act locally within the gonads. Usually inhibit FSH release; but also bind, ACTIVINS.

Fontanelle. Gap in the skeletal covering of the brain, either in the chondrocranium or between the dermal bones, covered only by skin and fascia. Present in newborn babies between frontal and parietal bones of the skull; closes at about eighteen months.

Food vacuole. Endocytic vesicle produced during PHAGOCYTOSIS.

Food web. The totality of interacting FOOD CHAINS with in a community of organisms. For stability of food webs.

Foramen. Natural opening (e.g. FORMEN MAGNUM OF SKULL, FORAMEN OVALE of foetal heart). Foramina in bones permit nerves and blood vessels to enter and leave.

Foramen magnum. Opening at back of vertebrate skull, at articulation with vertebral column, through which spinal cord passes.

Forebrain(prosencephalon). Most anterior of the three expansions of the embryonic vertebrate brain. Gives rise to diencephalon and telencephalon. Also the origin of the eyestalks. Associated originally with olfaction.

Forming face. (Of a Golgi body) the side on which cisternae of the Golgi body are assembled through fusion of vesicles derived from the endoplasmic reticulum or nuclear envelope.

Fossil. A fossil is evidence or the remains or prehistoric life. On some occasions as in the case of fossils in amber the organism's remains are preserved but usually the organisms' structures are replaced by various minerals. Tracks of prehistoric creatures also are classed as fossils.

Fossorial. Of animals adapted to digging, burrowing.

Fovea(Bot). Pit in the wall of palynomorphs, such as spores, pollen, or dinoflagellate cysts. (Zool). Depression in retina of some vertebrates, containing no rod cells but very numerous cone cells. May lie in a circular CONE-rich region termed the MACULALUTEA. Blood vessels absent, and no thick layer of nerve fibres between cones and incoming light as in rest of inverted retina. It is a region specialized for acute diurnal vision. Found in diurnal birds, lizards and primates, including man.

Frame shift mutation. A deletion or addition of a base in a region of DNA. The effect of frame shift mutations is to move every base beyond the mutation by one position meaning that when the mRNA that results from transcription is translated, the codons beyond the mutation point are different. This leads to a radically different sequence of amino acids from translation.

Fraternal twins. Dizygotic twins who develop as a result of simultaneous fertilization of two separate ova.Such twins are no more alike genetically than other siblings.

Freemartin. Female member of unlike sexed twins in cattle and occasionally other ungulates. Sterile, and partially converted towards hermaphrodite condition by hormonal influence of its twin brother reaching it through anastomisis of their placentae.

Free nuclear division. Stage in development in which unwalled nuclei result from repeated division of primary nucleus.

Free nuclear endosperm. Endosperm in which there are many nuclear divisions without cell division before cell walls start to form.

Free ze drying. Method of preserving unstable substances by drying when deeply frozen.

Freezeetching. Technique used in electron MICROSCOPY for examinig the outer surfaces of membranes.

Frequency-dependent selection. Form of SELECTION occurring when the advantage accruing to a character trait in a species population is inversely proportional to the trait's frequency in the population. When rate, it will be favoured by selection; when common, it will be at a disadvantage compared with alternative traits. two or more traits determied by the same genetic mechanism (locus, or loci) may thus coexist in the population in a condition of POLYMORPHISM.

Front. Term applied to leaf of a fern as well as divided leaves of other plants (e.g. palm).

Frontal bone A MEMBRANE BONE, a pair of which covers the front part of the vertebrate brain. Air spaces extend from nasal cavity into frontal bones of mammals.

Frontal lobe. Major part of the CEREBRAL CORTEX of the primate brain, including human's behind frontal bone. Has numerous connections with many parts of the brain.

Fructification. Reproductive organ or fruiting structure, often used in the context of fungi, myxomycetes and bacteria.

Fruit. Ripened ovary of the flower, enclosing seeds.

Fruit set. The production of a ripe fruit from an immature capel.

Frustule. Silica elements of the diatom cell wall.

Fruticose. Lichen growth from where the thallus is shrub-like and branched.

Fucosan vesicle. Refractive vesicles, usually around the nucleus, containing a tannin like compound in the brown algae. Also called physodes.

Fucoserraten. A sexual attractant produced by macrogamete in the brown algal genus Fucus.

Fucoxanthin. Xanthophyll pigment present with chlorophylls in various algal groups; e.g. PHAEOPHYCEAE CHRYSOPHYCEAE, PRYMNESIOPHYTA, BACILLARIOPHYCEAE.

Functional Group. A functional group is a an atom or a small group of atoms that attach to another molecule and alter the properties of that molecule. In biology we typically think of biological molecules as consisting of a backbone made of covalently bonded carbon atoms to which various functional groups are attached.

Fungi. The kingdom Fungi are generally multicellular heterotrophs. They are decomposers that obtain their nutrients by external digestion of complex organic matter. In addition to being eukaryotes, fungi usually have a cell wall made of chitin. Examples of Fungi include yeasts, molds, and mushrooms.

Fusiform initial(Bot). Meristematic cells of the vascular cambium. Vertically elongated cells, much longer than their width, appearing flatteed or brick-shaped in transverse section. Produce xylem and phloem cells having their long axes orientated vertically.

Fusion gene. The fusion of two adjacent protein-coding genes into a single one, by the deletion of the stopsignals of the first gene and the start-signals of the second gene, enabling translation to begin at the first one and carry on uninterruptedly until the end of the second one.

G

Galactose. A sugar found in lactose and many polysaccharides. It is an aldohexose, isomeric with glucose.

Gall bladder. A saclike extension of the bile duct that occurs in many vertebrates, situated between the liver lobes. It serves as a temporary store for bile, releasing it in response to food in the duodenum. The release of bile is controlled by the hormone cholecytokinin.

Gallery forest. A type of forest that grows alongside rivers and streams running through trophical grassland. The increased soil moisture is sufficient to support tree growth, which may be dense and multilayered, especially on alluvial nutrientrich soils of flood plains.

Gallstone. A hard ball of material formed in the gall bladder from surplus cholesterol, which precipitates in the bile. Gallstones may lodge in and obstruct the bile duct.

Galvani, Luigi (1737-98). Italian physiologist. In the late 1770s he observed that the muscles of a dead frog twiched when touched by two different metals. He concluded that the muscle was producing electricity, but this was later disproved. Galvani also invented galvanized iron and the galvaometer.

Gametangium. A structure in which sexual cells are produced, the term commonly being used with reference to reproduction in the algae and fungi.

Gamete. A haploid cell for use in reproduction to produce a diploid zygote upon fusing with another such haploid cell.

Gametogenesis. The formation of sex cells or gametes, i.e. ova or spermatozoa.

Gametophyte. A haploid multicellular plant that prod-ucts gametes by mitosis.

Gamopetalous. Describing a flower in which the petals are fused to form a corolla tube.

Gamosepalous. Describing a flower that possesses a calyx consisting of fused sepals.

Ganglion. A collection of nerve cell bodies, usually bound by a sheath or capsule. In vertebrates thc ganglia are located chiefly outside the central nervous system; in invertebrates ganglia occur along the major nerve cords and are the centres of nervous integration.

Ganoid scales. Hard ridged rhomboidal scales found in the skin of sturgeons and gars. The outer layer consists of ganoin, a calcareous substance secreted by the dermis; the inner layer consists of isopedin.

Gaseous exchange. The transfer of gases between an organism and the external environment in either direction. It occurs by diffusion across a concentration gradient and includes the exchange of oxygen and carbon dioxide in respiration and photosynthesis. Successful gaseous exchange requires a large surface area, as is provided by the alveoli of the lungs and the leaves of plants.

Gastric juice. An acidic mixture of inorganic salts, hydrochloric acid, mucus, and pepsinogens secreted by gastric glands in the stomach lining.

Gastric mill. A type of gizzard occurring in many crustaceans. It is situated in the enterior region of the stomach and consists of a set of bones and muscles that grind food particles. The food particles are then filtered by bristles in the posterior section of the stomach.

Gastrin. A hormone, produced by Gcells in the mucosa of the stomach and first part of the duodenum, that controls the release of gastric juice. The secretion of gastrin is stimulated by the presence of food in the stomach. It is one of the hormones that integrates and controls digestive processes.

Gastrodermis. The epithelial lining of the digestive tract of certain invertebrates, including the nematode worms and coelenterates.

Gastropoda. A class of molluscs that includes the snails, whelks, limpets, land and sea slugs, and conches. Molluscs have a well-developed head with tentacles, a large flattened foot, and a coiled twisted shell. They occupy marine, freshwater, and terrestrial habitates; in the terrestrial and some freshwater gastropods the mantle cavity acts as a lung instead of enclosing gills.

Gastrovascular cavity. The body cavity of the coelenterates, which has one opening functioning both as mouth and anus.

Gastrula. The stage in the developmet of an animal embryo that succeeds the blastula. It begins with the production of the primary germ layers and the embryo becomes converted to a cupshaped structure containing a cavity (the archenteron).

Gel. A lyophilic colloid that is normaly stable but may be induced to coagulate partially under certain conditions. This produces a pseudosolid or easily deformable jelly-like mass, called a gel, in which intertwining particles enclose the whole dispersing medium. Gels may be further subdivided into elastic gels and rigid gels.

Gemma. An organ of vegetative reproduction produced in mosses, liverworts, and certain pteridophytes, e.g. Lycopodium selago. They often form in groups in receptacles called gemma-cups and eventually become detached from the parent to form new plants.

Gene. A region of DNA ssociated with the expression of one or another form of a characteristic usually due to the protein coded for by the region of DNA. Alternate forms of a gene are called **alleles**.

Genecology. The study of population genetics in relation to enviroment.

Gene flow. The movement of alleles from one population to another via migration and interbreeding of migrant individuals.

Gene frequency. The proportion of an allele in a population in relation to other alleles of the same gene.

Gene library. A collection of cloned DNA fragments derived from the entire genome of an organism. The genetic material of the organism is first broken up randomly into fragments using restriction enzymes, for example. Then each fragment is cloned using a vector inside a suitable host, such as the bacterium E. coli. Particular genes or DNA sequences are identified by a suitable DNA probe.

Gene pool. The total number and variety of genes existing within a breeding population or species at a given point in time.

Generation time. The average time between the cell division of parent and daughter cells within a population of cells.

Generative nuclei. The two gametic nuclei found in the pollen tube. One fuses with the egg cell to form a zygote while the other either degenerates or, in certain angiosperms, fuses with the polar nucleus to give the primary endosperm nucleus.

Genetic code. A table displaying the possible messenger RNA codons and their corresponding amino acids and the stop codons.

Genetic drift. The loss of genes(alleles) from a population do to chance effects, specifically "sampling error" in small populations. The idea is that in small populations not all the different alleles at a particular locus will be passed on equally just by chance.

Genetics. The term coined by Bateson to describe the study of inheritance and variation and the factors controlling them. Today the subject has three main subdivisions-Mendelian genetics, population genetics, and molecular or biochemical genetics.

Genome. The complete set of genes in a cell. In a eukaryotic cell this may be taken to include the nuclear genes and genes in the mitochondria and other DNA bearing organelles.

Genotype. The genetic make-up of an organism, often with respect to a particular gene pair under study.

Genus. A collection of similar species. Genera may be subdivided into subgenera, and also, especially in plant taxonomy, into sections, subsections, series, and subseries. Similar genera are grouped into families.

Germ cell. One of a lineage of cells differentiated for the production of haploid cells for gametes or spores in plants by meiosis. In contrast somatic cells give rise to new cells by mitosis. In plants the situation gets confused.

Germ layer. In animals one of three tissue lineages that form during and are characteristic of an embryonic stage called **gastrulation;** Ectoderm, mesoderm, endoderm. These tissue layers are important because most of the organs in the body can be traced to one or another of these layers.

Germ line. The lineage of cells from which gametes arise, continuous through generations.

Gestation. The period of time between fertilization and birth in a viviparous animal. It is normally nine months in humans. The length of the gestation period tends to vary with the type of placenta and the size of the species; those with a highly developoed placenta, i.e. fewer layers and a smaller size have a shorter gestation.

Giant fiber (giant axon). A nerve fiber that has a relatively large diameter, enabling the rapid conduction of a nerve impulse. Giant fibres occur in many invertebrate groups and usually supply the muscles used in a protective response, such as the end-to-end contraction in earth-worms.

Gill. An evagination of an animal's body that serves as a respiratory surface.

Gill bar. One of a number of skeletal structures in the wall of the pharynx in fish that supports the tissue separating successive gill slits. They bear numerous fine filamets and are richly supplied with blood, into which oxygen diffuses from the water. Gill bars are also present in lower chordates, such as Branchiostoma.

Gill books. Respiratory organs of the king crabs, consistung of groups of thin plates attached to the abdominal appendages. They contain circulating blood. Their structure is similar to the lung books of terrestrial arachinds, indicating a evolutionary relationship between these groups.

Gill cleft. An opening through which water leaves the body of a cartilaginous fish after passing through the gills. There are normally six pairs of gill clefts situated laterally on the head of the fish. The anterior pair are usually smaller and situated close behind the eye.

Gill pouch. One of several pairs of compartments lying laterally to the respiratory tube in cyclostomes. They contain gill filaments.

Gill slits. Openings in the pharyngeal (throat) region of the alimentary canal of aquatic vertebrates, leading to the gills. In cartilaginous fish the first gill slit is modified as the spiracle. Traces of gill slits appear in the embryos of all vertebrates but persist only as the Eustachian the tube in adult terrestrial vertebrates.

Gingiva. The gum that covers the jaw bones and is continuous with the lining of the mouth. It consists of stratified squamous epithelium covering a dermal layer of connetive tissue containing nerves, lymph vessels, and many blood capillaries, which give a pink color to the gum. The gingiva is continuous with the alveolar membrane and with the pulp cavity through the pulp canal.

Ginkgo. A genus comprising only one species, G.biloba (maidenhair tree), this being the sole representative of the phylum Ginkgophyta. It is a deciduous dioecious tree with fanshaped leaves ad motile male sperms, native to the Far East.

Gizzard. A muscular compartment of the alimentary canal of many animals that is specialized for breaking up food. In birds the gizzard lies between the proventriculus and the duodenum and contains small stones and grit, which assist in breaking up the food when the gizzard contracts.

Glenoid cavity. The socket-shaped cavity in the scapula

that holds the head of the humerus in a ball-and-socket joint.

Glomerular filtrate. The fluid in the lumen of the Bowman's capsule of the nephron that has been filtered from the capillaries of the glomerulus. The glomerular filtrate has the same camposition as the plasma except that it does not contain any of the larger components, such as plasma proteins or cells.

Glomerulus. The first section of the kidney's nephron where filtration takes place. The glomerulus is made of a tight network of capillaries called the **glomerular capillaries** from which the blood filtrate is collected into the proximal collecting tubule of the nephron.

Glottis. The opening from the pharynx to the trachea. In mammals it also serves as the space for the vocal cords.

Glucagon. A hormone produced by the pancreas that stimulates the break down of glycogen and the release of glucose into the blood stream.

Glucan. Any polysaccharide composed only of glucose residues. e.g. starch and glycogen.

Glucose. A six carbon simple sugar(C6H12O6) commonly used as a source of energy by the organism. Glucose is produced by plants and either immediately used for cellular respiration or used to make polysaccharides such as starch or cellulose.

Glume. Either member of a pair of bracts that are found at the base of a spikelet of the grasses.

Glutamate. The anion of the amino acid glutamic acid. It functions as a neurotransmitter at excitatory synapses in the vertebrate central nervous system and at excitatory neuromuscular junctions in insects and crustaceans. In plans, glutamate is the initial acceptor molecule in the assimilation of the ammonium ion, combining with it to form glutamine in a reaction involving ATP.

Glycine. A sweet-tasting amino acid that, besides being a componet of proteins is the main inhibitory neurotransmitter for fast synapses in the spinal cord of vertebrates. Glycine is also required for opening of NMDA-type glutamate receptors.

Glycobiology. The study of carbohydrates and carbohydrate complexes, especially glycoproteins.

Glycerol. An alcohol with three hydroxyl groups. Glycerol is an oil alcohol that is an important component of fats and oils.

Glycogen. A polysaccharide produced by animals for short term energy storage. In humans and other mammals glycogen is stored in the liver and in the muscles. One of its uses is to help regulate blood glucose levels. Runners load up on "carbs" the day before a race to increase short term glycogen reserves in the skeletal muscles.

Glycolysis. The anaerobic breaking apart of glucose to yield ATP and 2 pyruvic acid molecules which happens in the cytoplasm of the cell.

Gnathostomata. A subphylum or superclass of chordates consisting of all vertebrates that possess jaws.

Gnotobiotic. Designating germ -free conditions, especially those in which experimental animals are inoculated with known strains of microo-rgaisms.

Goblet cell. A goblet-shaped cell, found in the epithelium of the intestine and respiratory system in mammals and in the epidermis of fish, that secretes mucus. Goblet cells have a wide top and constricted base and possess glycoprotein-containing vesicles.

Goitre. Enlargement of the thyroid gland resulting in a swelling of the neck. This may be caused by lack of iodine in the diet (which is required for the production of thyroid hormones), as the gland enlarges to compensate for this deficiency, or by hyperthyroidism.

Golgi body. A membranous organelle consisting of flattened sacs that serves as a way station and packaging site for materials synthesized by eukaryotic cells.

Gonad. Any of the usually paired organs in animals that produce reproductive cells. The most important gonads are the male testis, which produces spermatozoa, and the female ovary, which produces ova (egg cells). The gonads also produce hormones that control secondary sexual characteristics.

Grade. A group of organisms that share certain morphological characteristics but are not necessarily related in evolutionary terms.For example, all organisms that possess a coelom can be regarded as a grade. A grade can be contrasted with a clade, which represents phylogenetic lineage.

Gradualist model. The idea that species arise from preexisting species by means of a set of slow evolutionary transitions from one form to another.

Graft hybrid. A type of plant chimaera that may be produced when a part of one plant (the scion) is grafted onto another plant of different genetic constitution (the stock). Shoots growing from the point of union of the graft contain tissues from both the stock and the scion.

Gram. Symbol g. One thousandth of a kilogram. The gram is the fundamental unit of mass in *c.g.s. units and was formerly used in such units as the gram-atom, gram-molecule, and gram-equivalent, which have now been replaced by the mole.

Granulocyte. Any white blood cell that contains granular material and lysosomes in its cytoplasm. *Neutrophils, *basophils, and *eosinophils are examples of granulocytes.

Granulosa cells. Secretory cells in a *Graafian follicle that surround the oocyte. They have a function analogous to that of the Sertoli cells in the testis, supplying nutrients to the developing oocyte. After ovulation they form the corpus luteum.

Granum. In chloroplasts a series of flattened sacs each of which is called a thylakoid. These are important as the site of the light dependent reactions of photosynthesis.

Grazing. The consumption of vegetation,usually on *grassland, by animals, particularly cattle and sheep. Overgrazing can lead to desertification.

Grey matter. Part of the tissue that makes up the central nervous system of vertebrates. It is browngrey in colour, consisting largely of nerve *cell bodies, *synapses, and *dendrites. The grey matter is the site of coordination between nerves of the central nervous system.

Grooming. The actions of an animal of rearranging fur or feathers and cleaning the body surface by biting, scratching, licking etc., which is important for removing parasites and spreading oils over the body surface. In many mammals, especially primates, grooming between individuals has an important role in maintaining social cohesion.

Ground meristem. The meristem in plant shoots and roots, derived from the apical meristem, that gives rise to the cortex and pith (the ground tissues) in stems and the cortex and endodermis in roots.

Ground substance. The matrix of connective tissue, in which various cells and fibres are embedded. The ground substance of cartilage consists of chondrin.

Ground tissue. In plants one of the three main tissue types. Ground tissue makes up the bulk of the tissue in plants, with the possible exception of woody plants. Ground tissues have a number of functions including: support, gas exchange, starch storage, water storage,and photosynthesis.

Growth. An increase in the dry weight or volume of an organism through cell division and cell enlargement. Growth may continue throughout the life of the organism, as occurs in woody plants, or it may cease at maturity, as in humans and other mammals.

Guard cell. A specialized dermal cell in plants that is used to regulate the size of the pores(stoma) on the surface of plants through which gas exchange and water loss take place. Each stoma is surrounded by two lip like guard cells.

Guild. A group of species that exploit the same class of environmental resources in a similar manner.

Gums. Polysaccharid components, some pentose-rich, of

algal and plant cell walls; sometimes with oligosaccharide side chains, some residues of which may be acetylated. Include AGAR, ALGINIC ACID and CARRAGEENAN.

Gustation. The sense of taste.

Guttation. Excretion of water drops by plants through HYDATHODES, especially in high humidity, due to pressure built up within the xylem by osmotic absorption of water by roots.

Gut-associated lymphoid tissue (GALT). Any of various lymphoid tissues and structures that protect the digestive tract against infectious organisms and other ingested antigens. GALT includes the palatine *tonsils, adenoids (pharyngeal tonsils), appendix, Peyer's patches, and other clustered or diffuse lymphoid cells found throughout the gut wall.

Gymnosperm. A term no longer used in the formal schemes of classification, but still used informally. The term literally means 'naked-seeded plants', ovules and seeds lying exposed on their sporophyll (or analagous) surfaces, this being one of the principal characteristics of non-anthophyte seed plants. The four divisions with living species today are CONIFEROPHYTA, CYCADOPHYTA, GINKGOPHYTA and GNETOPHYTA.

Gynandromorph. Animal, usually an insect, which is a genetic MOSAIC in that some of its cells are genetically female while others are genetically male. Lose of an X-chromosome by a stem cell of an insect which developed from an XX zygote thus produces a clone of'male' tissue. Sometimes expressed bilaterally, one half of the animal being phenotypically male, the other female. Also occurs in birds and mammals.

Gynandrous (Bot). (Of flowers) having stamens inserted on the gynoecium.

Gynobasic (Bot). (Of a style) arising from base of ovary (due to infloding of ovary wall in development); e.g. white dead nettle.

Gynodioecious. Having female and hermaphroditic flowers on separate plants; e.g. thymes (THYMUS).

Gynoecium (pistil). Collective term for the carpels of a flower; i.e. the female components of the flower.

Gynogenesis. Condition where by a female animal must mate before she can produce parthenogetic eggs. In some triploid thelytokous animals (the salamanders Ambystoma, the fish Poeciliopsis) the sperm penetrates the egg to initiate cleavage but contributes nothig genetically.

Gynogenone. Diploid embryo with two maternal genomes produced by pronuclear transplantation.

Gynomonoecious (Bot). With female and hermaphroditic flowers on the same plant; e.g. many Compositae.

Gyrogonite. Lime encrusted, fossilized oogonia and encircling sheath cells (nucule) of the CHAROPHYCEAE. Earliest fossils occur in the Upper SILURIAN. Gyrogonites of extant species date from the Upper CARBONIFEROUS.

Gyrus. A fold (convolution) on the surface grey matter of the CEREBRAL CORTEX, between which occur deep grooves, or sulci. Both gyri and sulci are functionally differentiated and identified by names.

H

Habitat. The places where organisms of a species tend to live(e.g. stream bank, hard wood forest, prairie)

Habituation. A decline in organism's response to a stimulus with repeated applications of the stimulus.

Haem. Iron-containing PORPHYRIN, acting as PROSTHETIC GROUP of several pigments, including HAEMOGLOBIN, MYOGLOBIN and several CYTOCHROMES.

Haemagglutination. Clumping of red blood cells due to cross-linking of cells by antibody to surface antigens. Note to be confused with BLOOD CLOTTING.

Haemagglutinin. Glycoprotein product of INFLUENZA virus, associated, like neuraminidase, with the encapsulating host cell membrane and involved in attachment to host cells. Antigenic variation in haemaglutinin is responsible for new epidemics of the virus, against which earlier antibodies are ineffective.

Haemerythrin. Reddish-violet ironcontaining respiratory pigmet of sipunculds, one polychaete, priapulids and the brachiopod Lingula. Prosthetic group is not a porphyrin, the iron attaching directly to the protein. Always intracellular.

Haemocoele. Body cavity of arthropods and molluscs, containing blood. Continuous developmentally with the BLASTOCOELE. Unlike the COELOM, it nerve communicates with the exterior or contains gametes. Often functions as a hydrostatic skeleton. Contains haemolymph.

Haemocyanin. Copper-containing protein respiratory pigment occurring in solution in haemolymph of malacostracan and chelicerate arthropods and in many molluscs. Blue when oxygenated, colourless when deoxygenated.

Haemolysis. Rupture of red blood cells (e.g. through osmotic shock) with release of haemoglobin.

Haemostasis. Several homeostatic mechanisms maintaining blood in a fluid state, and within blood vessels. Includes BLOOD CLOTTING and FIBRINOLYSIS.

Hair cell. A mechanoreceptor that fires more frequently as sensitive tuffs at its end are bent. Hair cells are found in the inner ears of vertebrates and the lateral lines of fish. Hair cells are important in our ability to hear and maintain balance.

Hair follicle. A tubular pocket, formed by an ingrowth of epidermal cells into the dermis, enclosing the root of a hair. At the lower end, the cells are modified to produce hair. Muscles attached to the outside of the follicles can erect the hairs to increase thermal insulation. Nerve endings attached to the follicles can detect when objects make contact with the hairs. Sebaceous glands open into the follicle.

Hallux. The first digit of the hindfoot of tetrapods; it forms the big toe in humans. In the typical pentadactyl limb it contains two phalanges, however there are reductions and modifications to this general plan and in some mammals, e.g. the rabbit, it is absent. It is directed backwards in most birds as an adaptation to perching.

Halophyte. A plant that grows in soils with a high concentration of salt, as found in salt marshes. Examples are species of Spartina.

Halosere. A series of successional stages leading to a climax, originating in a saline area.

Haltere. One of a pair of club-shaped structures protruding from the sides of the thorax of flies. They are highly modified hind wings and vibrate rapidly during flight to provide information for the maintenance of balance.

Haplobiontic. Describing life cycles in which only one type of somatic body is formed, which may be either haploid or diploid. Haplobiontic is thus a collective term for haplontic and diplontic.

Haploid. Refers to a cell having one of each type of chromosome. Chromosomes(and genes) not in homologous pairs singly as in a gamete.

Haplodiploid. Organisms where one sex is diploid and the other sex is haploid. The females are diploid, the males haploid in all such known cases. Honeybees are a good example. The queen and workers are female and diploid, the males usually haploid.

Haplont. A haploid organism that represents the vegetative stage in life cycles in which diploidy is restricted to the zygote. Haplontic life cycles are typical of the filamentous green algae.

Haplontic. (Of a LIFE CYCLE) in which there is no diploid mitosis, but in which haploid mitosis does occur.

Haplorhine. The Suborders Haplorhini and Strepsirhini are the two sister groups of living primates. Haplorhines, lacking a RHINARIUM, include the tarsiers and anthropoids (platyrrhines and catarrhines).

Haplostele. A type of protostele having a solid strand of stele with the xylem on the inside encircled by phloem, pericycle, and endodermis.

Haplotype. A haploid genotype. The gametes produced by a normal outbred diploid individual will be of a variety of haplotypes.

Hapten. Molecule binding specifically to an antigen-binding site on an antibody molecule or lymphocyte receptor, but without inducing any immune response.

Haptonasty. A nastic movement in response to contact.

Haustorium. A specialized outgrowth of certain parasitic plants. e.g. fungi, that penetrates into and withdraws food material from the cells of the host plant.

Heat. A kind of kinetic energy carried by atoms or molecules in constant random motion. Be careful not to confuse heat with temperature. For instance, two rooms may both be at 27 degrees Celsius, but if the second room has twice the volume, the room will contain twice the heat of the first room.

Heartwood. The hard central region of a tree trunk made up of xylem vessels that are no larger involved in water transport. Such vessels are often blocked by substances (e.g. resins and tannins) that give the wood a darker color.

Helophyte. A perennial marsh plant that has its over-wintering buds under water.

Helper T cell. A lymphocyte in the immune system that stimulates both the cell mediated and the antibody mediated parts of the immune system, stimulating the production of both effector and memory T and B cells.

Heme. An iron-containing porphyrin that is the prosthetic group in hemoglobin, myoglobin, and cytochromes.

Hemerythrin. A red oxygen-carrying blood pigment similar to hemoglobin in containing iron and found in various invertebrates.

Hemicrytophyte. A perennial plant, usually non-woody, with its over-wintering buds at soil level. The buds are protected by the soil or surface litter.

Hemin. The hydrochloride form of heme. Hemin is the crystalline form in which heme can be isolated and studied in the laboratory. The iron present is the trivalent state. Hemin can be made to crystalize by heating hemoglobin gently with acetic acid and sodium chloride. A variety of crystal forms are known.

Hemizygous. Describing genetic material that has no homologous counterpart and is thus unpaired in the diploid state. Both single genes and chromosome segments may be hemizygous; for example, the X chromosome in the heterogametic sex, and whole chromosomes in aneuploids.

Hemocyanin. A blue copper-containing blood pigment found in many mollusks and arthropods. Hemocyanin is the second most abundant blood pigment after hemoglobin and functions similarly in acting as a oxygen-carrier in the blood.

Hemolysis. The release of hemoglobin from red corpuscles due to rupture of the cell membrane. It may be caused by such factors as toxins and incompatible blood transfusion.

Hemopoiesis. The formation of blood cells. In the fetus hemopoiesis occurs in the spleen and liver; in the adult it occurs in the bone marrow (erythrocytes and polymorph white cells) and lymphoid tissue (lymphocytes and monocytes).

Heparin. A substance that prevents blood clotting by neutralizing prothrombin and stopping the action of thrombin. It is present is tissues of mammals, and is secreted by some blood-sucking animals.

Herbivore. A plant-eating animal, especially one of the herbivorous mammals, such as cows, rabbits, etc. There may be various modifications associated with this diet, e.g. to the teeth and digestive system.

Heritability. In genetics heritability in the broad sense refers to the percentage of the total variation in phenotype in a population that is due to genetics as opposed to environmental influences.

Herpesvirus. One of a group of DNA containing viruses, about 100 nm in diameter, that cause such diseases as herpes and chickenpox. These viruses can remain latent in their host cells for long periods until triggered to produce symptoms of disease.

Herpetology. The branch of vertebrate zoology that is

concerned with the study of snakes.

Heterocercal tail. The type of tail found in the cartilaginous fish, in which the vertebral column extends into the tail, bending upwards as it does so. The caudal fin below the vertebral column is much larger than that above; when the fish is swimming the lower caudal fin contributes lift, preventing the fish from sinking (which it does immediately it stops swimming).

Heteroecious. Denoting rust fungi that require two host species to complete their life cycle. An example is Puccinia graminis, the stem rust of cereals and grasses, which overwinters on the barberry.

Heterogametic sex. The sex with dissimilar sex chromosomes, one (in mammals the Y chromosome) being shorter than the other (the X chromosome).

Heterograft. A type of graft from one organism to another of a different species.

Heterokaryosis. The presence of two or more nuclei with differing genotypes within a single cell. Fusion of fungal hyphae of differing genetic complements leads to heterokaryosis. Included fusion of different animal or plant cells is also effective in causing heterokaryosis.

Heteromorphism. The existence of more than one form, used especially with reference to life cycles in which the alternating generations are markedly different morphologically, as in ferms and jellyfish.

Heterophylly. Denoting plant species that have more than one form of foliage leaf on the same individual. where young leaves differ from adult leaves, as in ivy, this is termed developmental heterophylly.

Heterotroph. Refers to organisms that obtain their energy by complex organic compounds produced by other organisms. Animals and Fungi are technically heterotrophs.

Heterozygous. When both members of a gene pair in a diploid organism are not exactly identical but code for different expressions of the same characteristic.

Hexacanth. The sixhooked larva of a cestode worm. The

hooks are used by the larva for boring its way out from the intestine of the intermediate host and into the blood or lymph vessels. It is then carried in the blood or lymph to the muscles, where it develops into a bladderworm.

High-mobility group (HMG) proteins. Acid-soluble, non-histone nuclear DNABINDING PROTEINS with an HMG domain capable of bending or looping DNA in such a way as to form DNA supercoils. Some may have a role in immunoglobulin gene maturation.

High-throughput. A term, used especially in the contexts of GENOMICS and PROTEOMICS, to indicate that the assays used involve the simultameous study of very large numbers of genes, nucleic acid sequences or proteins, often requiring robotic sampling and handling techniques.

Hill reaction. Light-induced transport of electrons from water to acceptors such as potassium ferricyanide (Hill regents) which do not occur naturally, accompanied by the release of oxygen. During it, electron acceptors become reduced. Named after R. Hill, who studied the process in 1937 in isolated chloroplasts.

Hilum. Scar on seed coat, marking the point of former attachment of seed to funicle.

Hindbrain. Hindmost of the three expanded regions of the vertebrate brain as marked out during early embryogenesis, developing into the cerebellum and medulla oblongata.

Hippocampus. Part of the cerebral cortex, with a special role in learning (in which long-term POTENTIATION is involved). Affected by GLUCOCORTICOIDS.

Hirudinea. Leeches, Class of ANNELIDA. Marine, freshwater and terrestrial predators and temporary ectoparasites with suckers formed from modified segments at anterior and posterior ends. Most remain attached to host only during feeding. Hermaphrodite; embryo develops directly within cocoon secreted by chitellum.

Histamine. A local signaling molecule released by mast cells during an allergic reaction and as part of the the normal inflammatory responses of the body. Histamine acts on capillaries making them more leaky.

Histiocytes. Macrophages of the skin and subcutaneous tissues.

Histochemistry. Study of the distribution of molecules occuring within tissues, within both cells and intercellular matrices. Besides direct chemical analysis, it involves sectioning, STAINING and AUTORADIOGRAPHY.

Histocompatibility antigen. ANTIGEN (often cell-surface GLYCOPROTEIN) initiating an immune response resulting in rejection of an ALLOGRAFT.

Histogenesis. Interactive processes whereby undifferentiated cells from major GERM LAYERS differentiate into tissues.

Histology. Study of tissue structure, largely by various methods of STANING and MICROSCOPY.

Histone. Any one of a number of histadine rich proteins. These proteins are important in the nucleus of eukaryotic cells where there serve as a scaffolding for the DNA and are involved in gene expression.

Histone acetyltransferase. Any of several enzymes activating transcription by modifying particular amino-terminal tails of specific core histones by acetylating lysine residues in the histone tail domains. This destabilizes the nucleosome, allowing DNA-binding components of the basal transcriptional machinery better access to promoter elements.

Histone deacetylase. An enzyme removing acetyl groups from specific lysine residues in the tals of histones H3 and H4, causing gene repression by altering nucleosomal packaging.

HLA system (human leukocyte-associated antigen system). A group of histocompatibility antigens found on the surface of human body cells and encoded by the major histocompatiblity complex of genes. It is the most important system of self-antigens in humans, and is crucial in determining the compatibility of tissue grafts between different persons, for example.

Holdfast. In algae, the cell or organ that attaches the plant to the substrate. It is often disclike and is particularly prominent in the brown algae (e.g. Fucus).

Holoblastic. Describing the type of cleavage seen in certain eggs in which the first cleavages (animal-to-vegetal in orientation) divide the egg cytoplasm and yolk completely, as in sea urchins and frogs. Sometimes, as in most fishes, the cytoplasm but not the yolk is cleaved; this is not holoblastic cleavage.

Holocene (Recent). The present epoch in the geological time scale, being the second epoch of the Quaternary period, dating from the end of the last glaciation, about 10000 years ago, to the present day.

Holoenzyme. A catalytically active complex made up of an apoenzyme and a coenzyme. The former is responsible for the specificity of the holoenzyme whilst the latter determines the nature of the reaction.

Holophytic. The type of nutrition in which complex organic molecules are synthesized from inorganic molecules using light energy. It is another term for photoautotrophic.

Holothuroidea. The class of the Echinodermata that contains the sea cucumbers, which have a long cylindrical body showing secondary bilateral symmetry and covered with tough leathery skin in which the skeletal plates are reduced to spicules. There are no arms, but tube feet modified as food-catching tentacles surround the mouth. Other, tube feet are suckered for locomotion or pointed for burrowing.

Holozoic. Designating organisms that feed on other organisms or solid organic matter, i.e.most animals and insectivorous plants.

Homeostasis. The tendency of living things to actively maintain a constant internal environment.

Homeothermic. Refers to the ability to maintain a constant body temperature.

Homeotic genes. Genes involved in the overall organization of body plan and positioning of limbs in animals.

Hominid. A member of the primate family Hominidae, which includes modern humans as well as extinct forms found in great number and variety as fossils. Diagnostic features of fossil hominids include smaller canines, hyperbolic tooth rows, and smaller lower jaws than in fossil apes. The presence of stone tools associated with a fossil can also help in identification.

Homocercal tail. The type of tail found in adult bony fish, in which the vertebral column does not extend to the end of the tail and the caudal fin has two lobes of equal size.

Homodont. A type of dentition in which the teeth are all alike. This is found in such animals as frogs, in which all the teeth are similar small conical structures, cemented to the maxillae, premaxillae, and vomers of the upper jaw.

Homogametic sex. The sex with homologous sex chromosomes in mammals, designated XX.

Homogamy. The condition in flowers in which the anthers and stigmas ripen at the same time, so encouraging self-pollination. Homogamy occurs in the closed cleistogamous fowers that appear late in the season in certain plants.

Homograft. A type of graft between individuals of the same species.

Homoiothermy. The maintenance of the body temperature at a constant level, irrespective of environmental conditions. Birds and mammals are homoiothermic.

Homologous. Describing structures that, though in different species, are believed to have the same origin in a common ancestor. Thus the forelimbs and hindlimbs of all land vertebrates are said to be homologous, being constructed on the same fivedigit pattern.

Homologous Chromosomes. A pair of chromosomes that have corresponding genes in the same locations along the chromosome and that pair together to form tetrads during prophase I of meiosis.

Homoplastic. Describing similarity due to convergent or parallel evolution.

Homospory. The production of only one kind of asexual spore, which then develops into a hermaphrodite gametophyte. In the vascular plants the condition is seen in the ferns and Lycopodium species.

Homostyly. The usual condition found in plants in which the styles of all flowers of the same species are about same length. The term is not widely used, except as a comparison with heterostyly.

Homologous structures. Homologous structures are structures in different species that may have different functions and yet the structures have a common and deep developmental origin. Biologists infer that for organisms having homologous structures, the structures have a common evolutionary origin.

Homothallism. A condition found in algae and fungi in which each thallus is self-compatible. Homothallic species may produce distinctly different sizes of gametes and are thus effectively hermaphrodite.

Homozygous. When both members of a gene pair in a diploid organism are identical and code for the same expressions of a characteristic. Contrast **heterozygous.**

Hormone. A chemical messenger that in animals is produced by endocrine glands and then travels through the blood stream to have an effect on target cells. The term is also used for plants to refer to chemical messengers in general.

Host. An organism used as a source of nourishment by another organism, the parasite, which lives in or on the body of the host. In a definitive host the parasite reaches sexual maturity. In an intermediate host the resting stage or yung of the parasite are supported.

Humerus. The long bone of the upper arm of tetrapod vertebrates. It articulates with the scapula (shoulder blade) at the glenoid cavity and with the ulna and radius (via a condyle) at the elbow.

Humoral. Relating to the blood or other body fluids. For example, humoral immunity is immunity conferred by the antibodies present in the blood, lymph, and tissue fluids.

Humoral immune system. That part of the immune system concerned with the production of free **antibodies** from effector B cells and also the production of memory B cells via clonal selection.

Hyaluronic acid. A glycosaminoglycan that is part of the ground substance of connective tissue. Hyaluronic acid is a major component of articular cartilage and skin, helping in tissue repair and the lubrication of joints. It also plays a role in cell movement and proliferation and may contribute to the growth of certain tumours. Hyaluronidases break down hyaluronic acid.

Hyaluronidase. Any of a family of enzymes that break down hyaluronic acid, thereby decreasing its viscosity and increasing the permeability of connective tissue. Hyaluronidases are used in medicine to increase the absorption and diffusion of drugs administered by injection or application.

Hybrid. The offspring of a mating in which the parents differ in at least one characteristic. The term is usually used of offspring of widely different parents, e.g. different varieties or species. Hybrids between different animal species are usually sterile, as is the mule (a cross between a horse and a donkey).

Hybridoma. A type of hybrid cell that is produced by the fusion of a tumour cell (a myeloma cell) with a normal antibody-producing B cell. The resulting hybrid cell line is able to produce large amounts of normal antibody, which is described as monoclonal as it results from a cloned cell line.

Hybrid zone. A zone that exists between the populations of two related species, whose geographical ranages overlap, which contain hybrids resulting from matings between the two species. The hybrids, which have a reduced fertility, will eventually act as a barrier between further interspecific mating and hence will restrict gene flow between the two species.

Hydration shell. A group of water molecules that collects around a charged or polar ion, atom or molecule in solution. Hydration shells help to keep oppositely charged ions in solution by preventing the ions from from recombining. They are also important in keeping large molecules such as some proteins in solution or in suspension.

Hydrochloric acid. A strong acid, HCI, that is produced by oxyntic cells in the wall of the stomach and forms a constitues of gastric juice. Hydrochloric acid is required for the conversion of pepsinogen to pepsin in the lumen of the stomach and kills various microorganisms that enter with food.

Hydrocarbon. An organic compound consisting solely of carbon and hydrogen.

Hydrogen bond. A hydrogen bond is an electrostatic attraction between hydroxyl (OH) parts of a molecule and other charged parts of the same or different molecules. For example the negatively charged oxygen end of one molecule is attracted to the positively charged hydrogen ends of near by water molecules, hence the term hydrogen bond.

Hydrogencarbonate (bicarbonate). A salt of carbonic acid in which one hydrogen atom has been replaced; it thus contains the hydrogencarbonate ion.

Hydroid. A specialized elongated water-conducting cell found in the cortex of certain mosses. Hydroids are aligned end to end; at maturity they lose their cytoplasm and their end walls partially break down, becoming permeable to water and forming a rudimentary vessel.

Hydrolase. Any of a class of enzymes that catalyse the addition of water to, or the removal of waterfrom, a molecule. Hydroclases play an important role in the construction and breakdown of storage materials, such as starch.

Hydrogen ion pump(proton pump). A protein that uses the energy from electrons being carried along an electron transport system to pump hydrogen ions from one side of a cell membrane to another. This sets up an electrochemical gradient necessary for the production of ATP.

Hydrophilic. Literally means water loving and refers to the fact that hydrophilic molecules are attracted to water. This is because hydrophilic molecules have charged or polar molecular groups as part of their structure. Hydrophilic molecules can be recognized because they either dissolve in water or attract water to them.

Hydrophily. A rare form of pollination in which pollen is carried to a flower by water. It occurs by one of two methods. In Canadian pondweed the male flowers break off and float downstream until they contact the female flowers. In Zostera, a marine species, the filamentous pollen grains are themselves carried in the water.

Hydroponics. A commercial technique for growing certain crop plants in culture solutions rather than in soil. The roots are immersed in an aerated solution containig the correct proportions of essential mineral salts. The technique is based on various water culture methods used in the laboratory to assess the effects of the absence of certain mineral elements on plant growth.

Hydrophobic. Literally water fearing. More precisely this term refers to non polar molecules that because of their lack of charge, are neither repelled by or attracted to water. The term arises from the tendency of oil to separate itself from water in a mixture of oil and water. But the oil is not repelled by the water, rather since it has no charge, it can only associate with itself.

Hydrostatic skeleton. A series of fluid filled compartments found in many soft bodied invertebrates that use water pressure to maintain the organism's form. In some invertebrates, such as the earthworm, the hydrostatic skeleton is essential for locomotion.

Hydrotropism. The growth of a plant part in response to water. Roots, for example, grow towards water in the soil.

Hydroxyl group. A functional group consisting a hydrogen atom bonded to an oxygen atom. Hydroxyl groups are polar, and thus compounds with hydroxyl groups tend to dissolve in water.

Hygroscopic. Describing a substance that can take up water from the atmosphere.

Hymenoptera. An order of insects with two pairs of filmy wings and with biting mouth parts. The females have a well developed ovipositor and the males are usually haploid. In all cases hymenoptera have a larval stage which does not resemble the adult. Ants, bees, wasps are all in this order.

Hypertonic/Hypotonic. Hypertonic is a relative term referring to a solution with a greater concentration of solute(greater tonicity) than another solution. The second solution is considered **hypotonic** to the first one. These terms are important because in osmosis the diffusion of water across the cell membrane is going to be from the hypotonic side to the hypertonic side.

Hypha(ae). In fungi, a thread like structure consisting of cells one after the other. A mass of hyphae is called a **mycelium** and is the main part of most fungi.

Hypothalamus. A region of the brain involved in emotions, regulation of parts of the autonomic nervous system, and providing the link between the endocrine system and the nervous system by its influence on the pituitary gland.

Hypothesis. An hypothesis is an "educated guess" made by a scientist concerning the why or how of an observation made about the natural world. Creationists take note: an hypothesis is NOT a **theory**.

Hypoxia. A deficiency of oxygen in body tissues, which can result from livng in an oxygen-deficient environment, inadequate inspiration, or deficiency of red blood cells or haemoglobin.

Hzone. The region of a striated muscle fibre that contains only thick filaments. The H zone appears as a lighter and in the middle of the dark *A band at the centre of a *sarcomere.

I

Ice Age. A period in the latter part of the Pleistocene characterized by successive coolings and warmings of the earth. In at least four major glaciations, ice caps spread south from the Arctic and north from the Antarctic. Large areas of Britain, Europe, and North America were covered by ice from the North. The cause of the Ice Ages is not known, but it is assumed that others will occur in the future.

Ichthyology. The branch of vertebrate zoology that is concerned with the study of fishes.

Ichthyosauria. The only order of the extinct subclass of reptiles, the Ichthyopterygia, which lived from the Triassic to the Cretaceous and are known as the fishlizrds. Ichthyosaurus, common in the Jurassic, was a large predaceous marine reptile with a long snout, numerous teeth, a streamlined shark-like body, four paddleshaped limbs, and dorsal and caudal fins. Ichthyosaurs were probably ovoviviparous and never left the water.

Identical twins. Two offspring, produced during one birth, resulting from the division of a single fertilized egg. They are of the same sex and otherwise genetically identical, but may differ because of differences in nutrition, injuries, etc., either before or after birth. Identical triplets, quards, and quins are known, but multiple births in human beings usually result from the simultaneous fertilization of several eggs.

Idioblast. Any specialized plant cell that is dispersed among cells of a different kind. Idioblasts may contain a variety of materials, e.g. tannins, oils, crystals, and waste products. Isolated sclereids can be called idioblasts.

Idiotype. Antigenic constitution of the variable (V) region of an immunogloubin molecule.

IgD. Low titre immunoglobulin found attached to a CELL membranes. Of uncertain function.

IgE. Low the immunoglobulin located on basophil and mast cell surfaces. Possibly involved in immunity to helminths; also involved in asthma and hay fever hypersensitivity.

IgM. Class of large pentameric immunoglobulin molecules largely confined to plasma. Produced early in response to infecting organisms, whose surface antigens are often complex.

Ileum. Region of mammalian small intestine closest to colon and developing from region occupied by embryonic yolk sac; not anatomically distiinct from JEJUNUM. Its numerous villi, intestinal glands with their characteristic PANETH CELLS and GOBLET CELLS, enable it to serve as the major digesting and absorbing region of the mammalian alimentary canal.

Ilium. One of a pair of bones that form the dorsal part of the tetrapod pelvic girdle; they are the fanshaped part of the hip bones in humans. Each ilium is fused at its posterior side to the processes of the sacral vertebrate.

Imago. The final or adult stage in the life cycle of an insect. Unlike the earlier stages, the imago can fly and reproduce.

Immediate-early gene. Gene which is rapidly and transiently induced by a variety of extracellular stimuli. An example is c-fos.

Immunization. Process rendering an animal less susceptible to infection by pathogens, to toxins, etc. May confer active IMMUNITY through use of VACCINE; or passive immunity through injection of appropriate anitobides.

Immunocompetence handicap. A theory proposing that, in vertebrates at least, males 'honestly' signal their parasite resistance. It is debatable, because of testosterone's oft-assumed dual role; on the one hand its effects on secondary sexual characteristics and on the other its compromising effects on the immune system. According to the theory, only the fittest males are able to express traits attractive to females and still withstand parasitic infections.

Immunofluorescence. Use of antibodies, with a fluorescent marker dye attached, in order to detect whereabouts of specific antigens by formation of antibody-antigen complexes which show up on appropriate illumination. Antibody with such a fluorescent dye attached is serving as a primary antibody ; but if the antibody is itself unlabelled but serves as a target for a labelled secondary antibody then a stronger signal is achieved.

Immunogen. Any substance that can induce an immune response.

Immunoglobulin (Ig) superfamily. A large glycoprotein superfamily including ANTIBODIES and their membrane-bound isotypes; CELL RECEPTORS, lymphocyte Fc receptors, the CD2, CD4 and CD8 ACCESSORY MOLECULES and MHC molecules.

Immunological memory. Process whereby a CELLS and T CELLS exhibit accelerated responses when re-exposed to antigen owing to the presitence for many years of MEMORY CELLS of both kinds. Thucidides, describing the plague of Athens in 430BC, noted that the 'same man was never attacked twice', while the 19th-century Danish physician Panum noted that protective immunity was sustained in the absence of chronic exposure to measles virus.

Immunological synapse. Term coined to describe the interface between a T cell and either an ANTIGEN-PRESENTING CELL or B cell, which includes a minute gap into which cytokines, among other molecules, are secreted.

Immunophilins. Proteins serving as receptors for the principal immunosuppresant drugs. They interface with signal transduction systems in the cell, notably those involved in CALCIUM SIGNALLING and phosphorylation.

Implantation. Attachment of mammalian BLASTOCYST to wall of uterus prior to further development, placenta formation, etc. In humans the blastocyst is small and penetrates the endometrium, passing into the subepithelial connective tissue. This involves breaking of JUNCTIONAL COMPLEXES between endometrial cells, and proteolytic enzymes may be secreted by the TROPHOBLAST to achieve this.

Imprinting. Imprinting is a kind of learning that takes place during certain critical periods of an organism's life during which rapid and often irreversible fixation on presented stimuli happens. For instance many birds respond to the first organism they see upon hatching as they would to their mother with often comical results.

Inbreeding depression. Increase in proportion of debilitated or inviable offspring consequent upon INBREEDING, Extensively documented in captive plats and animals, examples have been slow to accumulate from wild populations.

Incisor. Chiseledged tooth of most mammals, occurring at the front of the dentary. Primitively three on each side, of both upper and lower jaws. Gnawing teeth of rodents and tusks of elephants are modified examples. Used for ripping, gnawig, cutting and pulling.

Inclusion granule. Microscopically visible bodies produced in the cytoplasms of many plant and animal cells, sometimes in the nucleus, as a result of viral infection. Often consist largely of virions, which may form crystals.

Incomplete dominance. A mode of inheritance in which the heterozygote has a phenotype that is intermediate between the phenotypes of either homozygotes. For instance for snap dragon flowers, if one homozygote is red, the other white, then the heterozygote will be pink. Incomplete dominance usually arises if one gene does not express a product and its other allele expresses an insufficient amount of product to mask the first allele.

Incomplete flower. Flower which lacks one or more of the kinds of floral parts, i.e. lacking sepals, petals, stamens or carpels.

Incus. One of the mammalian EAR OSSICLES, homologous with the quadrate bone of other vertebrates.

Indehiscent. (Of fruits) not opening spontaneously to liberate their seeds; e.g. hazel nuts.

Independent assortment. The random alignment and

subsequent separation of pairs of homologous chromosomes at the equator of the cell during metaphase I and anaphase I of meiosis. This process is important in **recombination** of the genetic material found in the gamete or spore producing organism.

Indeterminate growth. Unrestricted or unlimited growth; continues indefinitely.

Indeterminate head. Flat-topped INFLORESCENCE possessing sterile flowers with the youngest flowers in the centre.

Indigenous. Indicating an organism native to a particular locality of habitat.

Individualistic concept. The concept of the community as an association of species that occur together simply because of similarities in requirements and not as a result of a long co-evolutionary history.

Inducible enzyme. Enzyme synthesized only when its substrate is present.

Indusium. Membranous outgrowth from undersurface of leaves of some ferns, covering and protecting a group of developing sporangia.

Induced fit model. The induced fit model says that the sites on enzymes or receptor molecules where substrate molecules will alter their shape slightly to accommodate the substrate molecules. This is in contrast to the old lock and key model of enzyme activity which held that the enzyme active site had a set and rigid shape. The induced fit model is important because it suggests that enzymes don't have to perfectly "fit" with the substrate in order to operate and thus evolution has plenty of leeway in terms of new enzyme variants evolving.

Inductive reasoning. Reasoning from a series of specific observations to a set of one or more general principles.For example, Darwin used sets of observations of the fossil record, the distribution of organisms, and the structure of organisms to infer natural selection that natural selection is a general concept helping to explain the diversity of life on Earth.

Inferior. Describing a structure that is positioned below or lower than another structure in the body. For example, in flowering plants the ovary is described as inferior when it is located below the other organs of the flower.

Inflorescence. A particular arrangement of flowers on a single main stalk of a plant. There are many different types of inflorescence, which are classified into two main groups depending on whether the tip of the flower axis goes on producing new flower buds during growth or loses this ability.

Infradian rhythm. A biorthythm whose periodicity is less than a day in length. Numerous cellular processes have a although whether these infradian rhythms of cell function are entrained with any environmental cues is often hard to establish.

Infraspecific. Occurring within a species. For example, infraspecific variation is the variation occurring between individuals of the same species.

Ingestion. The taking of food into the organism and physical processing before digestion.

Inguinal. Of, relating to, or situated in the groin. For example, the inguinal canal, which contains the spermatic cord, lies in the abdominal cavity of a male fetus.

Inheritance. The transmission of particular characteristics from generation to generation by means of the genetic code, which is transferred to offspring in the gametes.

Initial. One of a group of cells that divides to produce the cells of a plant tissue or organ. The cells of the apical meristem, cambium, and cork cambium are initials.

Innate behaviour. An inherited pattern of behaviour that appears in a similar form in all normally reared individuals of the same sex and species.

Inner compartment of mitochondrion. The central area of the mitochondrion, sometimes called the matrix and where the Kreb's cycle happens.

Innervation. The supply of nerve fibres to and from an organ.

Innominate artery. A short artery that branches from the aorta to divide into the subclavian artery and the right carotid artery.

Innominate bone. One of the two bones that form each half of the pelvic girdle in adult vertebrates. This bone is formed by the fusion if the ilium, ischium and pubis.

Inoculation. The placing of a small sample of microorganisms or any other type of cell into a culture medium so that the cells can grow and proliferate.

Inoculum. A small amount of material containing bacteria, viruses, or other microorganisms that is used to start a culture.

Insect ivora. An order of small mainly nocturnal, mammals that includes the hedgehogs, moles, and shrews. They have long snouts covered with stiff tactile hairs and their teeth are specialized for seizing and crushing insects and other small prey. The insectivores have changed very little since they evolved in the Cretaceous period, 130 million years ago.

Insectivore. An animal that eats insects, especially a mammal of the order insectivora.

Insight learning. Modification of an organism's behavior brought about by combining information received from the environment in new ways to solve problems. Supposedly characteristic of human beings and a relatively small group of other vertebrates.

In silico. Describing biological processes or experiments that are simulated by a computer program.

Instar. A stage in the larval development of an insect between two moults. There are usually a number of larval instars before metamorphosis.

Instinct (Instinctive behavior). An instinct is a simple or complex set of behaviors that are innate rather than learned.

Insulin. A protein hormone produced by the beta cells of the pancreas' islets of Langerhorns and that is involved with the regulation of blood glucose levels. Specifically insulin promotes the uptake of **glucose** and the formation of **glycogen** in the liver and muscles.

Integration. The coordination within the brain of separate but related nervous processes. For example, sensory information from the inner ear and the eye are both necessary for the sense of balance. These stimuli must be integrated by the brain not oly with each other but also with various motor nerve, which coordinate the muscles that control posture.

Intercalary. Occurring between differentiated tissues. For example, intercalary meristem, which is not part of the apical meristem, occurs in the internodes of grasses and enables longitudinal growth of the stem.

Intercellular. Located or occurring between cells.

Intercostal muscles. The muscles located between the ribs, surrounding the lungs. Comprising the superficial external intercostal muscles and the deep internal intercostal muscles, they play an essential role in breathing.

Intergenic suppressor. A point mutation that negates or lessens the effects of another mutation in the same gene. For Example, the effects of a primary frameshift mutation may be suppressed by a second mutation in which the deletion or insertion of a nucleotide occurs.

Interleukins. A series of local chemical signals involved in the immune system and that activate the production of cytotoxic T cells and promote the increased production of helper T cells.

Intermembrane space. The region in the mitochondrion that is between the outer and inner membranes of the organelle. The intermembrane space is important because the mitochondrion concentrates hydrogen ions in this area as part of electron transport phosphorylation.

Interneuron. A neuron that transmits information from at least one neuron to at least one other neuron. Interneurons in humans are characteristic of the central nervous system.

Internode. In plants, the region of the stem between where the leaves are attached.

Interoceptor. A receptor that detects stimuli from the internal environment of an organism. Chemoreceptors that detect changes in the levels of oxygen concentration in the blood are examples.

Interphase. That part of the eukaryotic cell life when the chromosomes are not visible using a light microscope and when the cell is doing its every day function. The DNA actually duplicates during interphase and thus the chromosomes go from being unduplicated to duplicated.

Interspecific. Occurring between members of different species. The term is applied, for example, to some types of competition and communication.

Interstitial fluid. Fluid that is in the tissues: more literally, in the spaces that are in between the cells.

Intervertebral disc. Any of the discs of cartilage that separate the bones of the vertebral column. The intervertebral discs allow the vertebral column a certain degree of flexibility and they also absorb shock.

Intestine. The protein of the alimentary canal posterior to the stomach. Its major functions are the final digestion of food matter from the stomach, the absorption of soluble food matter, the absorption of faeces.

Intracellular. Located or occurring within cells.

Intraspecific. Occurring between members of the same species. The term is applied, for example, to some types of competition and communication.

Intron. A segment of RNA transcript that is edited out by the cell and that stays in the nucleus. Introns appear to have a role in controlling gene expression in eukaryotes. Prokaryotes do not have introns. Contrast **exon**.

Intussusception. The insertion of new cellulose fibres in the space between existing fibres in the wall of an elongating plant cell. This type of growth results in increasing the surface area of the cell wall.

Inulin. A polysaccharide, made up from fructose molecules, that is stored as a food reserve in the roots or tubers of many plants, such as the dahlia.

In utero. Describing any event occurring in the uterus of a mammal during pregnancy.

Invertebrate. Any animal that lacks a vertebral column. Invertebrates include all nonchordate animals as well as the more primitive chordates.

In vivo. Describing biological processes as they are observed to occur in their natural environment,i.e. within living organisms.

Involuntary. Not under the control of the will of an individual. Involuntary responses by muscles, glands, etc., occur automatically when required; many such responses, such as gland secretion, heartbeat, and peristalsis, are controlled by trhe autonomic nervous system and effected by involutionary muscle.

Iodine. Symbol 1. A dark violet nonmetallic element that is required as a trace element by living organisms; in animals it is concentrated in the thyroid gland as a constituent of thyroid hormones.

Ion. An atom or molecule with an unequal number of protons and electrons. Thus the atom or molecule has either a net positive or a negative charge.

Ionic bond. A bond between two atoms involving a complete transfer of electrons. Usually ionic bonds involve atoms of elements on the far left hand side of the periodic table and atoms of elements near the right hand column of the periodic table.

Ipsilateral. Of, relating to, or affecting the same side of the body.

Iron. Symbol Fe. A silvery malleable and ductile metallic element that is the fourth most abundant element in the earth's crust. It is required as a trace element by living organisms. Iron is an important constituent of haemoglobin and the cytochromes, being stored in the liver in the form of ferritin. In animals deficiency of iron results in a form of anaemia.

Irradiation. Exposure to any form of radiation; often exposure to ionizing radiation is implied.

Ischium. The most posterior of the three bones that make up each half of the pelvic girdle.

Isoelectric point. The pH of a medium at which a protein carries no net charge and therefore will not migrate in an electric field. Proteins precipitate most readily at their isoelectric points; this property can be utilized to separate mixtures of proteins or amino acids.

Isogamy. Sexual reproduction involving the production and fusion if gametes that are similar in size and structure. It occurs in some protists, e.g. certain protozoans and algae.

Isomerase. Any of a class of enzymes that catalyse the rearrangement of the atoms within a molecule, thereby converting one isomer into another.

Isomers. Two molecules that have the same molecular formula (e.g. C6 H12 O6) but a different structure. Glucose and fructose are isomers of each other.

Isotonic. Two aqueous solutions are considered isotonic is they have the same concentration of solutes. Contrast **hypertonic**.

Isotope. An atom with a different number of neutrons but the same number of protons than another atom. Isotopes, thus can be said to have the same atomic number but different mass number. All isotopes of the same element have the same chemical properties. However some are radioactive. Isotopes are useful in medicine, biochemistry and in paleontology.

Itaconic acid. A product of the fermentation of carbohydrates by strains of the filamentous fungus Aspergillus.

J

Jaw. The part of the vertebrate skeleton that provides a support for the mouth and holds the teeth. It consists of the upper jaw and the lower jaw. Agnathans lack jaws.

Jejunum. The part of the small intestine between the duodenum and the ileum.

Jugular vein. One of a pair of veins in mammals, each with a internal ad external portion, that carry deoxygenated blood away from the head and neck. They unite with the subclavian veins and lead into the anterior venae cavae.

Jugular vein. A paired vein in the neck of mammals that returns blood form the head to the heart. It joins the subclavian vein at the base of the neck.

Junctional complex. A site at which there is direct contact between neighboring animal cells, for example between epithelial cells bordering a lumen. There are at least four tyes of special contact between cells; an attachment plaque or desmosome; an adhesive zone; a tight or occluded junction; and a gap or intermediate junction.

Jurassic. The middle period of the Mesozoic era, 215-145 million years ago. During the Jurassic dinosaurs were becoming large and abundant and bony fishes were also evolving rapidly. Fossils of the earlist known bird Archaeopteryx and of the first mammals are found in the late Jurassic.

Juvenile hormone. A hormone secreted by insects from a pair of endocrine glands close to the brain. It inhibits metamorphosis and maintains the presence of larval features.

K

Kainate. An analogue of glutamic acid obtained from the red alga Digenea simplex that is a specific agonist for a subset of glutamate receptors- the kainate receptors.

Karyotype. A picture of the chromosomes of a cell showing the chromosomes in order by size and shape to facilitate chromosome identification.

Karyogamy The fusion of nuclei or nuclear material that occurs during sexual reproduction.

Karyogram. A diagram representing the characteristic features of the chromosomes of a species.

Karyokinesis. The division of a cell nucleus.

Karyorrhexis. A stage of cell death that involves fragmentation of a cell nucleus. The nucleus breaks down into small dark beads of damaged chromatin. This usually leads to further dissolution of the nucleus, where upon the damaged chromatin gradually fades.

Karyotype. The number and structure of the chromosomes in the nucleus ofa cell. The karyotype is identical in all the diploid cells of an organism.

Keel. The projection of bone from the sternum of a bird or bat, to which the powerful flight muscles are attached. The sterna of flightless birds lack keels.

Kelp. Any large brown seaweed or its ash, used as a source of iodine.

Keratin. A fibrous protein found in hair, horns, hooves, feathers, scales and nails of of various vertebrates.

Ketone bodies. Substances such as acetoacetate and hydroxybutyrate produced mainly in the liver from acetyl co-enzyme A, itself an oxidation product of fatty acids, released for use by peripheral tissues as fuel. The metabolic pathway is termed ketogenesis.

Keratinization. The process in which the cytoplasm of the outermost cells of the mammalian epidermis is replaced by keratin. Keratinization occurs in the stratum corneum, feathers, hair, claws, nails, hooves, and horns.

Kilo. Symbol k. A prefix used in the metric system to denote 1000 times. For example, 1000 volts = 1 kilovolt (kV).

Kilobase. Symbol kb. A unit used at the molecule level for measuring distances along nucleic acids, chromosomes, or genes, equal to 1000 bases.

Kilogram. Symbol kg. The SI unit of mass defined as a mass equal to that of the international platinumiridium prototype kept by the International Bureau of Weights and Measures at Sevres, near Paris.

Kinase. An enzyme that catalyzes the transfer of a phosphate group from ATP to another substrate.

Kinesis. A Kinesis is an undirected change in movement in response to an environmental stimulus. Unlike a taxis, a kinesis is not oriented toward or away from the stimulus.

Kinetin. A purine, probably not occurring naturally, but acting as a CYTOKININ in plants.

Kinetochore. A region of specialized proteins at the centromere that serves as an attachment point for spindle microtubules during mitosis and meiosis.

Kingdom. Taxonomic category with the greatest generally commonly employed, inclusive of divisions. Controversy has occured over the number of kingdoms to employ. Today most recognize five kingdoms: MONERA, PROTISTA, FUNGI, ANIMAL and PLANTAE.

Kin selection. A Kin selection is a kind of natural selection in which individuals increase the number of their genes left to future generations by providing aid to relatives who also share some of the same genes.

Klinostat. A device used in experiments to test the influence of gravity on the growth movements of plants. It consists of a motor that slowly rotates a drum inside which seedings are attached. This prevents any single part of the seedings from receiving uninterrupted gravitational stimulation and results in horizontal growth of the seedlings.

Kranz anatomy. The arrangement of palisade mesophyll cells in a circle around the vascular bundle of C4 plants.

Krebs, Sir Hans Adolf (1900-81). German-born British biochemist, who emigrated to Britain in 1933, working at Sheffield University before moving to Oxford in 1954. Krebs is best known for the Krebs cycle, the basis of which he discovered in 1937. Details were later added by Fritz Lipmann, with whom Krebs shared the 1953 Nobel Prize for physiology or medicine.

Kreb's cycle(Citric acid cycle). A series of chemical reactions that takes a two carbon residue from acetyl CoA and strips high energy electrons and hydrogen ions(protons) from the residue. These electrons and protons are used to make ATP and the starting material for the cycle is regenerated to pick up more two carbon residues. The term **citric acid cycle** refers to the fact that citric acid results when the two carbon residue attaches to the cycle's starting material.

Krummholz. Region between the alpine and tree lines, where trees are dwarfed and deformed owing to serve environmental conditions, particularly wind.

Kupffer cells. Specialized macrophages that dispose of old blood cells and particulate matter. Kupffer cells, named after Karl Wilhelm von Kupffer, are found in the bloodstream and in the liver, attached to the walls of the sinusoids.

L

Labial. Referring to LABIUM, or to lip-like structure.

Labiate process. Tube or opening through the valve wall of a diatom with an internal flattened tube or longitudinal slit often surrounded by two lips.

Labrum. Plate of exoskeleton hinged to front of the head in some arthropod groups and serving to enclose a space in front of the actual mouth. Found in insects and crustaceans. Trilobites had a similar structure, but placed ventrally on the head.

Labyrinthodontia. Subclass of extinct amphibians found as fossils from Upper Devonian to Upper Triassic. Generally believed to have has rhipidistian ancestors.

Lac operon. DNA sequence in the genome of the bacterium Escherichia coli comprising an operator, promoter, and three structural genes, transcribed into a single mRNA, encoding enzymes involved in lactate uptake and metabolism.

Lactate(lactic acid). An organic acid produced from fermentation by a wide range of bacteria and the skeletal muscles of our bodies under anaerobic conditions.

Lacteal. Lymph vessel draining a VILLUS of vertebrate small intestine. After digestion, reconstituted fats are released into the lacteal as CHYLOMICRONS.

Lactose. A disaccharide made from glucose and galactose. Lactose is commonly known as milk sugar because of it's abundance in milk. To taste lactose, try condensed milk which you can buy in the store as a canned product.

Lacuna (Zool). Any small cavity, such as those containing bone or cartilage cells.

Lamellipodium. Sheet-like extension, or flowing pseudopodium, of the leading edges of many vertebrate cells during locomotion, some forming attachments with the substratum, others carried back in waves. Many give rise to microspikes.

Lamina. (1) Sheet or plate; flat expanded portion of a leaf or petal. (2) In brown algae , expanded leaf-like portion of the thallus.

Lamina propria. Loose connective tissue of a MUCOUS MEMBRANE binding the epithelium to underlying structures and holding blood vessels serving the epithelium.

Laminarin. Storage polysaccharide product of the brown algae, occurring as oil-like liquid contained in a membrane-bound sac surrounding the pyrenoid but outside the CHLOROPLAST.

Land use ecology. The study of the role and impact of ecological factors on land use patterns, productivity and managment, in the past as well as the present.

Lasso cell. Cell type characteristic of CTENOPHORA, whose tentacles are armoured with these sticky thread-cells for capturing prey. Do not penetrate prey, unlike nematocysts of cnidarians.

Latent Heat. Heat that is stored by a particular substance. We are interested in latent heat because water stores more heat per gram than any common substance. The fact that water stores so much heat helps to moderate the earth's climate.

Lateral meristems. Meristems giving rise to secondary tissue; the vascular cambium and cork cambium.

Larva. An immature form of an animal. Insects, the larvae typically will be quite different in appearance and feeding preferences from the adult. Example: caterpillars are the larvae of butterflies and moths.

Laver. General name given to the edible dried preparation made from the red alga Porphyra.

Leaf base. Usually the expanded portion of the leaf, attached to the stem.

Leaf scar. Scar marking where a leaf was formerly attached to the stem.

Leaf sheath. Base of a modified leaf, forming a sheath around the stem.

Leaf trace. (1) Vascular bundle extending between vascular system of stem and leaf base; where more than one occurs, each constitutes a leaf trace. (2) Vascular supply extending between vascular system of stem and leaf base, consisting of one or more vascular bundles, each known as a leaf trace bundle.

Lectotype. Specimen or other component of original material, selected to serve as a nomenclatural type when no HOLOTYPE was designated at the time of publication, or as long as it is missing.

Lemma. Lower member of pair of BRACTS surrounding grass flower, enclosing not only the flower but also the other bract.

Lentic. (Of freshwaters) where there is no continuous flow of water, as in ponds, lakes.

Lenticel. An opening in the surface of a twig though which gas exchange takes place.

Lentivirus. Any of a group of 'slow' retroviruses inducing neurological impairment and chronic pneumonias. Include visna virus of sheep and HIV.

Lepidosauria. Dominant subclass of living reptiles; possess DIAPSID skulls and overlapping horny scales covering the body. Includes the orders Rhyncocephalia.

Leptocephalus. Oceanic larva of European eel. Migrates over 2,000 miles across Atlantic from breeding site near West Indies to European fresh waters, where it becomes adult. Transparent.

Leptoma. Thin area in wall of gymnophyte pollen, through which the pollen tube emerges.

Leptome. Photosynthate-conducting cell, approaching phloem in structure and function, found in bryophytes.

Leptosporanglate. (Of vascular plant sporangia) arising from a single parent cell and possessing a wall of one layer of cells. Spore production is low in comparison with EUSPORANGIATE type.

Leptotene. Stage in first prophase of MEIOSIS during which chromosomes are thin and attached at both ends to the nuclear membrane. DNA has already replicated but each chromosome appears as one thread, sister chromatids being closely apposed.

Learning. Learning is the ability of an organism to modify its behavior based on past experience. All animals appear to be capable of at least some simple learning as are some single celled organisms. Whether certain animals take advantage of their ability to learn is another matter.

Leucoplast (amyloplast). An organelle related to chloroplasts and that stores starch. The while appearance in the ground tissue of potato is due to leucoplasts. In actuality the leucoplast starch grains are typically clear, not white as implied by the name.

Leukotrienes. Lipid product of arachiodonic acid removal from membrane phospholipids and its subsequent modification. They constrict bronchial airways, stimulate chemotaxis of white blood cells and mediate INFLAMMATION by increasing permeabilities of small blood vessels.

Leydig cells. Groups of relatively scanty cells in the interstices between seminiferous tubules of the vertebrate testis responsible for steroid production. Have unusually large smooth endoplasmic reticulum. Testosterone output is synergistically enhanced by PROLACTIN and LUTEINIZING HORMONE.

Libriform fibre. Xylem fibre having thick walls and greatly reduced pits.

Licensing. A process which ensures that chromatin is available for a further round of DNA replication only after its passage through mitosis.

Lichen. A symbiotic association between fungi and one or more types of photosynthetic organism. The latter night be an algae or a cyanobacteria.

Ligases. A series of enzymes that tie or connect pieces of DNA together based on complementary ends of the DNA strands. These are important enzymes for genetic engineering because they allow scientists to splice genes into other sections of DNA, for example into opened bacterial plasmids.

Light. Electromagnetic radiation, typically that which is visible to either our eyes or the eyes of other animals. Light is not matter but pure kinetic energy.

Light dependent reactions. The first steps in photosynthesis in which light energy is captured and then converted to ATP and NADPH. These in turn supply energy for the rest of photosynthesis. Oxygen is produced as a waste material by the light dependent reactions, at least under current conditions.

Light independent Reactions. The Calvin cycle and other related reactions in photosynthesis where by carbon dioxide is fixed from the atmosphere and hydrogen ions and electrons are added to produce sugars, specifically PGAL.

Ligament. Form of vertebrate CONNECTIVE TISSUE joining bone to bone. Yellow elastic ligaments consist primarily of elastic fibres and form relatively extensible ligaments joining vertebrate, and true vocal cords; collagenous ligaments bycontrast consist largely of parallel bundles of collagen and resist extension.

Ligase. ENZYME catalysing condensation of two molecules and involving hydrolysis of ATP or another such triphosphate. DNA LIGASE is much used in GENE MANIPULATION, as well as forming part of DNA REPAIR MECHANISMS.

Lignocellulose. Major chemical component of wood. Valuable resource, not least of energy as when converted to methane or alcohol in techniques of BIOTECHNOLOGY.

Limb bud. Circular bulge on the neurula surface during vertebrate embryonic development, the somatic mesenchyme cells of which will proliferate and differentiate to form the limb elements. A ridge along its anterior margin is a major signalling centre for the developing limb, keeping the mesenchyme dividing and generating the anterior-posterior limb axis.

Linkage. The tendency of genes located at different loci on the same chromosome to stay together during independent assortment more often than would be expected if the genes were on separate chromosomes.

Linnean hierarchy. Arrangements of organisms into TAXA; forming nested sets, with KINGDOM the highest taxonomic category and SPECIES the lowest.

Linoleic acid. ESSENTIAL FATTY ACID of mammals, making up to 20% of the total fatty acid content in their triglycerides.

Lipid. A lipid is any number of diverse organic compounds all of which are characterized by having long hydrocarbon skeletons and by being generally nonpolar. This means that lipids do not usually dissolve in water and are thus considered hydrophobic. However, the interactions between lipids and water are important in the organization of plasma membranes. Lipids do dissolve in non-polar solvents such as ether or benzene. Examples of lipids include steroids, fats and oils and phospholipids.

Lipolysis. Hydrolysis of lipids, particularly of triglycerides.

Liposome. Artificially produced spherical lipid bilayers, as m or more in diameter, which can be induced by segregate out of aqueous media. Their selective permeabilities to organic solutes and the subsequent reactions which can occur within them have led some to propose a similar structure as a cell prototype.

List. Cellulose extension of cell wall in some armoured dinoflagellates, usually extending out from the cingulum and/or sulcus.

Lithotroph. Autotrophic bacterium obtaining its energy from oxidation of inorganic substances by inorganic oxidants; the terminal hydrogen acceptor in respiration is always inorganic.

Littoral. Inhabiting the bottom of sea or lake, near the shore. From shore to 200 m in the sea; to 6-10 m in lakes, depending upon the extent of rooted vegetation.

Living fossil. Any organism whose closest relatives are extinct and that was once itself thought to be extinct. An example is the coelacanth, a primitive fish that was common in the Devonian era, the first recent living specimen of which was discovered in 1938.

Loam. A fertile soil that is made up of organic matter mixed with clay, sand, and silt. Loams differ in their ratios of clay, sand, and silt, which influences which types of plants they can support.

Lobopod. (1) A blunt-ended pseudopodium found in certain protozoans. (2) A number of the phylum Lobopodia.

Locule. Compartment, cavity or chamber. In ASCOMYCOTA, chambers containing ASCI; in flowering plants, cavity of the ovary where ovules occur; in diatoms, a chamber within the frustule having a constricted opening on one side and a VELUM on the opposite side.

Local signaling molecules. Molecules a released by cells not in a gland that generally travel through the interstitial fluid and have their effect locally. Contrast hormones are released into the blood stream. Examples of local signaling molecules include histamine and prostaglandin's, as well as neurotransmitters.

Locus. The specific place or position of a gene on a chromosome.

Lodicule. Either of two small scales situated at the base of the floret of grasses. They may represent the reduced perianth and be involved in the opening of the floret at the time of pollination.

Logarithmic scale. A scale of measurement in which an increase or decrease of one unit represents a tenfold increase or decrease in the quantity measured. Decibels and pH measurements are common examples of logarithmic scales of measurement.

Logistic growth. A type of population growth in which the population starts out growing exponentially but as resources become limiting, growth rate becomes zero and the population is at a long term equilibrium. Of course in real populations there's no guarantee of a painless approach to any sort of equilibrium.

Lomentum. A type of dry dehiscent fruit formed from a single carpel but divided into one-seeded compartments by constrictions between the seeds. Legumes and siliquas can be divided in this way.

Long day plant. A plant in which flowering can be induced or enhanced by long days, usually of more than 12 hours of daylight. Examples are spinach and spring barely.

Loop of Henle. A hairpin shaped region of the kidney's nephron that is involved with the resorption of salt and water. Longer loops of Henle are associated with more efficient water conservation. Hence desert animals have longer loops of Henle than do their non desert counterparts.

Lophophore. An organ characteristic of aquatic invertebrates of the phyla Bryozoa, Phoronida, and Brachiopoda that functions in filter feeding. It consists of a ridge of hollow tentacles bearing cilia, which waft food particles into the mouth.

Lophotrochozoa. A clade of protostome animals, based on molecular systematics, that includes the molluscs and annelid worms, together with the nemertines, bryozoans, and other wormlike phyla.

Lorenz, Konrad Zacharias. Austrian ethologist who studied medicine, becoming a lecturer at Vienna in 1937. Watching the behaviour of birds on his private estate, he made his studies of imprinting. For this work he shared the 1973 Nobel Prize for physicology or medicine with Karl von Frisch and Niko Tinbergen.

Lumbar vertebrate The vertebrate in the region of the lower back. They occur below the thoracic vertebrate and above the sacral vertebrate. In mammals they bear processes for the attachment of back muscles.

Lumen. 1. The space enclosed by a vessel, duct, or other tubular or saclike organ. The central cavity of blood vessels and of the digestive tract are examples. 2. Symbol lm. The SI unit of luminous flux equal to the flux emitted by a uniform point source of 1 candela in a solid angle of 1 steradian.

Lung book. The respiratory organ of some arachnids. Lung books occur in pairs on the ventral side of the abdomen. They consist of leaflike folds of ectoderm sunk into pockets having slitlike openings at the adbominal surface.Gaseous exchange occurs by diffusion through the ectodermal folds.

Luteal phase. The phase of the oestrous cycle that occurs after ovulation. During this phase the corpus luteum secretes oestrogens and progesterone, which prepare the uterine wall to receive a fertilized egg.

Luteinizing hormone. A hormone, secreted by the enterior pitutary gland in mammals, that stimulates in males the production of sex hormones by the interstitial cells of the testes and in females ovulation, progesterone synthesis, and corpus luteum formation.

Lyase. Any of a class of enzymes that catalyse either the cleavage of a double bond and the addition of new groups to a substance, or the formation of a double bond.

Lymph. The colourless liquid found within the lymphatic system, into which it drains from the spaces between the cells. Lymph resembles blood plasma, consisting mostly of water with dissolved salts and proteins. Fats are found in suspension and their presence varies with food intake. The lymph eventually enters the bloodstream near the heart.

Lymph heart. Any of a series of muscular pumping structures that occur in the major lymphatic vessels of certain lower vertebrates and maintain a flow of lymph around the body. Many animals lymph hearts; in these the flow of lymph is maintained by a series of muscle contractions and valves.

Lymph node. A mass of lymphoid tissue, many of which occur at intervals along the lymphatic system. Lymph in the lymphatic vessels flows through the lymph nodes, whih filter out bacteria and other foreign particles, so preventing them from entering the bloodstream and causing infection. The lymph nodes also produce lymphocytes. In humans, major lymph nodes occur in the neck, under the arms, and in the groin.

Lymphocyte. An of a number of cells associated with either specific or non specific aspects of the body's defense against foreign invaders.

Lysogenic pathway. A complex pattern of virus reproduction in which viral genetic material inserts itself into the host cell's genetic material. The host cell then reproduces, reproducing virus material along with its own genetic material. The result is a number of generations of host cells with the viral materal incorporated into their own genetic material. At some point an environmental trigger (perhaps stress) causes the viral genetic material to instruct the cells to produce new viral particles as in the **lytic pathway**.

Lymphoid tissue. The type of tissue found in the lymph nodes, tonsils, spleen, and thymus. It is responsible for producing lymphocytes and therefore contributes to the body's defence against infection.

Lysergic acid diethylamide. A chemical derivative of lysergic acid that has potent hallucinogenic properties. It occurs in the cereal fungus ergot and was first synthesized in 1943. ISD acts as an antagonist at serotonin receptors.

Lysigeny. The localized disruption of plant cells to form a cavity in which secretions accumulate. Examples are the oil cavities in the leaves of circus trees.

Lysimeter. An instrument used to measure the loss of water from an area of land covered with vegetation. Water that evaporates from both the soil and from the plats can be determined.

Lysosome. An organelle containing digestive enzymes for intracellular digestion. In multicellular animals, lysosomes are important for programmed cell death(apopsis) that is a part of organismal development. Without cell death during development we would, at the very least, have webbed fingers.

Lytic pathway. A type simple pattern of virus reproduction in which a virus invades a cell, causes the cell to produce more viruses. When the cell is full of viruses it breaks open or lyses, releasing the new viruses.

Lysozyme. An antibacterial enzyme widely distrubuted in body fluids and secretions, including tears and salvia. It disrupts the polysaccharide components of bacterial cell walls, leaving them susceptible to destruction.

M

Macro-evolution. The processes related to the patterns observed in biogeography and in the fossil record related to patterns of evolution in groups of related species. A familiar example is adaptive radiation. Note that macroevolution is not strictly the same thing as speciation and even many texts are confused on this point.

Macromolecule. Molecule of very high molecular weight, characteristic of biological systems, e.g. proteins, nucleic acids, polysaccharides, and cmplexes of these.

Macronutrients. Substances required in large amounts for plant growth; e.g. nitrates, phosphates, sulphates, calcium and magnesium.

Macrophage. Literally a "big eater". A white blood cell involved in the release of histamine, eating anything that it detects as being foreign, and finally in presenting antigens, or pieces of antigens called epitopes, to other cells in the immune system.

Mallophaga. Biting lice; bird lice, feather lice. Exopterygotan insects, ectoparasitic on birds and occasionally on mammals. Flatened, with tersal claws and reduced eyes. Cannot pierce skin but bite small particles of FEATHERS or hair. Include hen louse, Menopon.

Malpighain corpuscle. In vertebrate KIDNEY, a glomerulus and its associated Bowman's capsule.

Malpighain layer. Innermost layer of epidermis of vertebrate skin, next to dermis. An active region of MITOSIS, non-stem cells being pushed to the surface, ageing and becoming cornified. Its cells often contain the pigment melanin, darkening the skin as a protection against ultraviolet light.

Maltose. Disaccharide sugar composed of two glucose molecules bonded in an a glycosidic linkage. Formed by the enzymatic degradation of starch by AMYLASES. Occurs e.g. in germinating seeds such as barley, and during digestion in animals.

Mandible. (1) Of vertebrates, the lower JAW. (2) Of insects, crustacea and myriapods, one of the first pair of MOUTHPARTS, usually involved in biting and crushing food and heavily sclerotized.

Mannan. Polysaccharide, composed of mannose units and occurring in cell walls of some algae and yeasts.

Mannitol. A 6-carbon sugar alcohol universally present in the brown algae in which D-mannitol is the accumulation product of photosynthesis.

Mannoglycerate. Saccharide storage product in some red algae.

Marginal meristem. MERISTEM located along margin of leaf primordium and forming the blade.

Marginal placentation. Attachment of ovules to carpel margin.

Marginal value theorem. A proposed theoretical model relating to the decision of a predator to leave patches of prey which it has depleted, it states that the predator should leave all patches at the same rate of prey extinction, namely the maximum average overall rate for that environment as a whole.

Marsupials. A group of mammals with young that leave the mother's uterus at a very early stage and finish their development in a pouch. Kangaroo and possum are two examples.

Marsupium. Pouch of many marsupials and spiny anteater. Fold of skin supported by epipublic bone of pelvic girdle, forming pouch containing mammary glands or similar structure, into which newborn are placed. Young marsupials attach there to teats, or lick milk in the case of teatless Exhidna.

Masseter muscle. Muscle running from inside the zygomatic arch and inserting on the outside and rear of the mammalian lower jaw, pulling jaws forward and up and assisting in side-to-side motions.

Mass flow. Hypothesis for explaining TRANSLOCATION of material in phloem of vascular plants.

Mass cell. Granular LEUCOCYTE derived from MYELOID TISSUE, often associated with mucosal epithelia. When not in connective tissue, dependent upon T CELLS for reproduction. Granules in cytoplasm contain SEROTONIN, HEPARIN, HISTAMINE and TUMOUR NECROSIS FACTOR-o; released when allergen cross-links the lgE molecules bound to plasma membrane. Involved in many allergles, but also in Immunity to parasites.

Mass number. The mass number of an atom is the mass of the atom's protons plus neutrons plus electrons.

Matter. Anything that takes up space and has mass. Electrons, protons, and anchovies are all matter. Light is not.

Maternal gene. Term sometimes used specifically for a gene responsible for a MATERNAL EFFECT.

Maternal inheritance. Characters inherited through the female line only. Not all genes are transmitted via nuclear chromosomes. Evolution of ansiogamy means that the female parent may contributes more genetically to its offspring than does the male parent.

Maxillule. Paired crustacean mouthpart, lying behind the mandibles and in front of the maxillae. Usually a phyllopodium, passing food to the mouth.

MCM complex. Six proteins whose interactions with chromatin as a cell exists from mitosis licenses the DNA for replication.

Meatus. A passage or channel in the body, such as the exteral auditory meatus in birds, mammals, and some reptiles, which leads from the exteral opening of the ear to the eardrum.

Mechanoreceptor. A receptor that responds to a mechanical stimulus, e.g. touch, pressure, sound, etc.

Meckel's cartilage. A paired cartilage forming the lower jaw in cartilaginous fish, such as sharks, skates, and dogfish. In bony fish, reptiles, and birds it is ossified to form the articular bone. In mammals it persists as an ear ossicle, the malleus.

Median eye. An eye in the middle of the head, found in some crustaceans, such as the microscopic pond animal Cyclops. It is a simple light receptor. Some insects, such as the locust, have a median ocellus as well as a pair of compound eyes. The new Zealand lizard, Sphenodon, has a median third eye that is functional.

Medullated protostele. A type of protostele in which there is a central nonvascular pith surrounded successively by xylem, phloem, pericycle, and endodermis.

Medusa. A stage in the life cycle of cnidarians in which the body is shaped like a bell or inverted saucer wiith a fringe of tentacles around the rim and a mouth beneath. The medusa is the free-swimming dispersal stage of the life cycle; in scyphozoans it is the only form. Medusae have sex organs; sperms swim from the male to fertilize eggs in the female. The fertilized egg develops into a planula.

Megasporophyll. A leaf or modified leaf that bears the megasporangium. Simple megasporophylls are the fertile ligulate leaves of heterosporous lycopods. They are usually grouped in a strobilus that may also contain micro-sporophylls or vegetative leaves. The carpel of angiosperms and the ovuliferous scale of gymnosperms are modified megasporophylls.

Meiosis. A type of cell division in eukaryotes characterized by the reduction of chromosome number from the diploid to haploid number and by several processes of recombination so that the daughter cells have different combinations of genes. In animals meiosis leads to the production of **gametes**. In plants the products of meiosis are called **spores**. Contrast **mitosis**.

Melanism. The possession of a dark appearance due to the presence of a dark brown pigment, melanism.

Melanocyte-stimulating hormone. A peptide hormone produced by the anterior pitutary gland in vertebrates. It has a marked action on pigmentation in the skin of amphibians and reptiles, but its physiological role in mammals is unclear.

Mendelism. The theory of inheritance according to which characteristics are determined by particulate 'factors', or genes, that are transmitted by the germ cells. It is the basis of classical genetics, and is fouded on the work of Medel in the 1860s.

Meninges. The protective membranes that surrounded the brain and spinal cord in vertebrates. In humans and other mammals there are three; the stiff outer duramater, the arachnoid membrane, and the soft inner pia mater. The letter two are separated by the subarachnoid space, which is filled with cerebrospinal fluid.

Mericarp. A one-seeded dehiscent or indehiscent portion of a schizocarpic fruit. It is found for example in the Geraniceae, whose fruit, the regma, splits into five dehiscent mericarps. The cremocarp of the Umbelliferae splits into two indehiscent mericarps.

Meristele. A segment of a dictyostele formed by overlapping leaf gaps. A meristele contains all the tissues of a stele, usually arranged in a concentric pattern. The xylem is surrounded by a layer of phloem, and bounded by a pericycle and endodermis. It is seen in many club mosses and ferns.

Meroblastic. Describing the type of incomplete cleavage that occurs in very yolky eggs, in which the egg cytoplasm but not the yolk divides.

Mesarch. Denoting a stele or part of a stele in which the protoxylem is surrounded by metaxylem.

Mesoderm. The middle of the three embryonic tissue layers formed during an embryo's gastrulation.

Mesoglea. The layer of jelly-like material that separates and is secreted by the ectoderm and endoderm in sponges and cnidarians. It varies from a thin membrane to a thick gelatinous mass.

Mesophyll. The ground tissue found in the middle of the leaf, between the upper and the lower epidermis. Typically the mesophyll is divided between the palisade mesophyll, specialized for the light reactions of photosynthesis and the spongy mesophyll specialized more for gas exchange and the dark reactions of photosynthesis. In plants with fleshy(succulent) leaves, other mesophyll is specialized for water storage.

Mesophyte. A plant that is adapted to grow under adequate conditions of water supply. In drought conditions wilting is soon apparent as the plants have no special mechanisms to conserve water. Most angiosperms are mesophytes.

Mesothelium. The tissue, consisting of one or more layers of cells, that lines a coelomic cavity.

Mesozoic. The middle era in the most recent eon of the geological time scale, dating from about 230-66 million years ago. Known as the 'Age of Reptiles', it is divided into three main periods; the Triassic, Jurassic, and Cretaceous.

Messenger RNA(mRNA). RNA produced by transcription of DNA and that is destined to leave the nucleus to be translated as part of protein synthesis.

Metabolism. The set of all energy using and energy producing reactions within an organism; or the sum of all reactions that break down chemical compounds(for example digestion)and reactions that build complex compounds from simple compounds(for example protein synthesis).

Metabolite. A substance that takes part in a metabolic reaction, either as reactant or product. Metabolites are thus intermediates in metabolic pathways. Some are syntherized within the organism itself, whereas others have to be taken in as food.

Metabolic pathway. A sequence of chemical reactions involved in metabolism. Examples of metabolic pathways include glycolysis, the Kreb's cycle and the Calvin cycle.

Metacarpus. The collection of metacarpal bones forming part of the forefoot or lower forelimb in tetrapods; the palm of the hand in humans.

Metachronal rhythm. A pattern of movement shown by cilia, parapodia of certain polychaetes, etc., in which each beats one after the other in regular succession and gives the appearance of wave motion. A wave passing forwards may propel the surrounding medium backwards or the organism forwards.

Metanephridium. An excretory organ in many Annelida, consisting of a tubule that opens into the coelom by a ciliated funnel and conducts waste fluids to the exterior.

MHC marker. A protein found on the surface of the cells of our bodied that enables or cells to be recognized by the immune system as belonging to the body....or at least ignored by the immune system. Sometimes the immune system doesn't properly ignore these markers.

Microbody. Any of a class of cell organelles that typically are spherical vesicles, 0.2-1.5 um. bounded by a single membrane. Microbodies contain enzymes responsible for the oxidation of various materials and they originate from the endoplasmic reticulum. They include peroxisomes and glyoxysomes.

Microclimate. The local climate of a small area or of a particular habitat, which is different from the macro-climate of the larger surrounding geographical area.

Micro-evolution. A change in the genetic make-up of a population through time due to one of the agents of evolution. These are: natural selection, nonrandom mating, genetic drift, immigration, emigration and mutation.

Microfauna. 1. Animals that cannot be seen with the naked eye. They are normally observed with the aid of a microscope. 2. The animals that live in a particular microhabitat.

Microfilament. One of a number of cytoskeleton components made from the protein actin When associated with filaments of myosin these can contract and form the basis for cell movement including our muscle cells.

Microflora. 1. Plants and algae that cannot be seen with the naked eye. They are normally observed with the aid of a microscope. 2. The plants and algae that live in a particular microhabitat.

Micronutrient. A chemical element required by plants in relatively small quantities. Micronutrients are typically found in cofactors and coenzymes. They include copper, zinc, molybdenum, manganese, cobalt, and boron.

Microorganism. Any organism that can be observed only with the aid of a microscope. Microorganisms include bacteria, viruses, protists, and fungi.

Microphagous. Describing the method of feeding of those heterotrophic organisms that take in their food in the form of tiny particles. Filter feeding and ciliary feeding are examples of this type of feeding.

Microphyll. A type of foliage leaf in clubmosses and horsetails that has a single unbranched midrib. Such leaves are generally no more than a few millimetres long.

Microsome. A fragment of endoplasmic reticulum formed when cells or tissues are disrupted. Microsomes can be isolated by centrifugation and are commonly used to investigate the functional properties of endoplasmic reticulum, such as enzymic activity and protein synthesis.

Microspore mother cell. A diploid cell in plants that divides by meiosis to give rise to four haploid microspores. In flowering plants microspore mother cells are formed within the pollen sacs of the anthers by mitosis; the micro-spores they produce develop into pollen grains.

Microtubule. A hollow tube made from a helical formation of a protein called tubulin. Microtubules are important in cell division, as components of centrioles, cilia and flagella.

Microvillus. One of a number of minute finger-like projections on the free surfaces of epithelial cells. Microvilli are covered with plasma membrane and their cytoplasm is continuous with the main cell cytoplasm. Their purpose is to increase the absorptive or secretory surface area of the cell, and they are abundant on the villis of the intestine, where they form a brush border.

Micturition. The discharge of urine from the bladder. It is brought about by reflex contraction of the detrusor muscle after voluntary relaxation of the sphincter muscle at the junction of the bladder with the urethra.

Middle lamella. A thin layer of material, consisting mainly of pectins, that binds together the walls of adjacent plant cells.

Midgut. 1. The middle section of the alimentary canal of vertebrates, which is concerned with digestion and absorption. It comprises most of the small intestine. 2. The middle section of the alimentary canal of arthropods.

Milli. Symbol m. A prefix used in the metric system to denote one thousandth. For example, 0.001 metre = 1 millimetre.

Mimicry. The tendency of two species to closely resemble each other because such resemblance confers an advantage with respect to predators of the species. There are two main types of mimicry. In **Batesian mimicry**, a harmless creature has evolved to resemble a harmful or noxious creature. In **Mullerian mimicry**, two or more noxious(to the predators!) species have evolved to resemble each other.

Mineral salts. Inorganic salts that need to be ingested or absorbed by living organisms for healthy growth and maintenance. They comprise the salts of the trace elements in animals and the micronutrients of plants.

Mitochondrion(a). A DNA containing organelle found in most eukaryotic cells. Mitochondria are the sites of the Kreb's cycle and electron transport phosphorylation.

Mitosis. A type of cell (nuclear) division in eukaryotes characterized by the production of identical daughter nuclei. Typically the cytoplasm of the parent cell divides, a process called **cytoplasmic division** but this need not be the case. Mitosis is used for growth and repair of multicellular organisms and for asexual reproduction. Contrast **meiosis**.

Mixed tissue. Tissue containing more than one cell type, all originating from same group of stem cells in development. XYLEM and PHLOEM are examples.

Mixotroph. PHOTOAUTOTROPH capable of utilizing organic compounds in the environment; facultative heterotroph or facultative parasite may also refer to a mixotroph.

Modification. Methylase activity preventing or reversing host restriction. Specific bases of the phage DNA within target site of tthe restriction endonuclease are methylated. Nonheritable change.

Molar. Crushing back tooth of mammal, without milk tooth predecessor. Usaully has several roots and complicated pattern of ridges and projections on grinding surface.

Molecule. A chemical entity consisting of two or more atoms of the same or different elements chemically bonded together.

Monadelphous. (Of stamens) united by their filaments to form tube surrounding the style, e.g. in lupin, hollyhock.

Monera. One of the five currently recognized Kingdoms of life. These organisms have a cell wall, but lack a nucleus or other membrane bound organelles. The cells are called prokaryotic (pro = before; karyotic= seed(nucleus). Representative prokaryotes are the true bacteria, cyanobacteria and archebacteria. This kingdom, based on current research is likely to be broken up into several large kingdoms.

Monoamine oxidase. Enzymes (e.g. on the outer membrane of mitochondria) oxidatively removing the amine group of monoamines converting, e.g., noradrenaline to a glycoaldehyde.

Monocarpic. 1. Having one carpel per flower, as in Leguminoseae. 2. (Of plants) reproducing only once and then dying. Contrast POLYCARPIC.

Monochlamydeous (haplochlamydeous). (Of flowers) having only one whorl of perianth segments.

Monocot. Any of a group of angiosperms with a single seed leaf, leaf veins parallel, vascular bundles scattered throughout the stem and flower parts in multiples of three. Well known monocots include grasses, lilies, bamboo and orchids.

Monocolpate. Referring to a pollen grain with one furrow or groove through which pollen tube will emerge.

Monocyte. Largest of the kinds of vertebrate LEUCOCYTE. Can differentiate into MACROPHAGES and are the source of numerous GROWTH FACTORS, notably PDGF and interleukin.

Monoecious. (Of plants) having both maleand female repoductive organs on the same individual; in flowering plants, having unisexual, male and female, flowers on the same plant, e.g. hazel.

Monohybrid cross. A genetic cross where only one trait is under investigation. Usually these crosses start our with each parent being homozygous for different alleles of the same gene.

Monokaryon. A fungal cell, hypha or mycelium in which there are one or more genetically identical haploid nuclei. Characteristic of the early phase in life cycles of many of the BASIDIOMYCOTA.

Monoophyletic. Of a taxon or taxa originating from and including a single stem species and either including the whole CLADE so derived, or else excluding one or more smaller clades nested within it (a paraphyletic taxon).

Monooplanetism. In some PROTISTA (e.g. some oomycota), where a zoospore of only one type is produced.

Monopodium. An axis produced and increasing in length by apical growth; e.g. trunk of a pine tree.

Monosomy. Abnormal chromosome complement, one chromosome pair in an otherwise diploid nucleus being represented by just a single chromosome. An instance of ANEUPLOIDY. May arise by NON-DISJUNCTION. The norm in the heterogametic sex of thise animals with the XO/XX mode of sex DETERMINATION.

Monotremata. Monotremes. The only order of the mammalian subclass PROTOTHERIA. Molecular systematics links monotremes with marsupials.

Monotremes. A group of primitive mammals restricted to the Australian region that are characterized by laying eggs. The Platypus and the Echidna are the living representativcs of this group.

Morph One form of INFRASPECIFIC VARIATION; one of the forms of a species population exhibiting POLYMORPHISM, generally of a markedly obvious kind.

Morphogenesis. Literally the origin of form. The process by which an embryo develops from a single cell into a organized system of differentiated tissues. This involves a complex combination of genetic and environmental influences.

Morphological convergence. Structures in unreted organisms that have a similar appearance due to common evolutionary pressures. **Analogous** structures are evidence of morphological convergence.

Morphospecies. Species recognized by a museum taxonomist using conventional criteria. These may harbour morphologically indistinguishable sibling species.

Morula. Animal embryo during CLEAVAGE, at the stage when it is a solid mass of cells. Stage prior to the BLASTULA. Human embryos implant at this stage.

Motor neuron(effector neuron). A neuron that sends information from the central nervous system to a muscle, gland or both. Hence since they may enervate other effectors than muscle these neurons are more properly called effector neurons. Contrast with interneuron, sensory neuron.

Motor unit One motor neurone, its nerve terminals, and the skeletal muscle fibres innevated by them. There may be 200or more muscle fibres in each vertebrate motor unit in large muscles of the leg or trunk.

Mould. 1. Any superficial growth of fungal mycelium.

Frequently found on decaying fruit or bread. 2. Popular name for many fungi.

Moulting 1. For moulting in arthropods. 2. The periodic sheeding of FEATHERS in birds, and of hair in mammals.

Mucin The main constituent of mucus. It is a glycoprotein.

Mucous membrane. The tissue, in vertebrates, that lines many tracts that open to the exterior. It consists of surface epithelium containing goblet cells, which secrete mucus, and is underlaid by connective tissue.

Mucus. A slimy substance produced by goblet cells in mucous membrane of animals. It is viscous and insoluble, consisting mainly of glycoproteins. Its function is to protect and lubricate the surface on which it is secreted.

Muscle. Tissue consisting of elongated cells containing fibrils that are highly contractile.

Mutagen Any physical or chemical agent that induces mutation or increases the rate of spontaneous mutation. Chemical mutagens include ethyl methanesulfonate, which cause changes in the base pairs of DNA molecules, and acridines, which cause base pair deletions or additions. Physical mutagens include ultraviolet light, X-rays, and gamma rays.

Mutation. A change in the make-up of the genetic material of an organism. In multicellular organisms mutations may affect somatic (body) cells or sexual (the gametes) cells. The former may give rise to cancer while the latter may be passed on from one generation to the next providing the raw material for evolution.

Mutualism A type of symbiotic relationship where both partners benefit. An important mutualistic relationship involves the roots of trees and specialized fungi. This relationship which improves the absorption of nutrients by roots and provides food for the fungus is called a **mychorrhiza**.

Mycelium. In fungi, the mass of food absorbing cellular fibers(Hyphae) that make up the main part of the fungus. The fuzzy bread mold you might be familiar with is an example.

Mycetozoa. A taxon name used for slime molds in certain classifications.

Mycoprotein Any protein produced by a fungus or bacterium.

Myelinated nerve fiber. A nerve fiber that is surrounded by a fatty sheath. Most nerves of vertebrates consist of thousands of medullated fibres, which appear whitc because of the fatty sheaths.

Myelin Sheath. A protein wrapped around the axons of many neurons and produced by one of a number of specialized cells. For motor neurons, the myelin sheath is produced by Schawnn cells. The myelin sheath speeds up the transmission of nerve impulses down the length of the axon.

Myelocyte. A cell in the myeloid tissue of red bone marrow. Myelocytes are formed by cell division of precursor cells and they chage into granulocytes, which are released into the bloodstream.

Myoneme. A contractile fibril found in certain protoctists.

Myosin. A protein found in muscle cells that interacts with actin to bring about muscle contraction.

Myotome. The part of each of a vertebrate embryo that differentiates as a muscle block. The muscle myotomes remain segmental in fishes, but in terrestrial vertebrates they lose much of their original vertebrates they also much of their original pattern and buds from myotomes form muscles in limbs, etc.

Myxovirus. One of a group of RNA containing viruses that cause such diseases as influenza, mumps, measles, and rabies.

N

NAD (nicotinamide adenine dinucleotide). A derivative of nicotinic acid that acts as a coenzyme in electron-transfer reactions. Its role is to carry hydrogen atoms; the reduced form is written NADH.

NADP. Nicotinamide adenine dinucleotide phosphate; a coenzyme similar in its action to NAD.

Nasal cavity. A paired cavitry in the heads of vertebrates. It contains thin bones covered with a mucous membrane and it is lined with epithelium, some regions of which contain nerve endings sensitive to smells. In mammals the large area of mucous membrane warms and moistens air as it passes through on its way to the lungs. Hairs near the nostrils and mucus from the membrane filter dust and bacteria from the air.

Nastic. Undirected(usually) and reversible responses of plants to being touched. Nastic responses are undirected in the sense that the response does not bring about an orientation toward the touch. Examples of nastic response include leaf closings of mimosa plants when touched and the rapid closing of a Venus fly trap.

Natural killer cell. A large lymphocyte with prominent lysosomes that attaches to the surface of virus-infected cells and secretes substances that puncture the target cells membrane. This allows the entry of other substances that trigger the death of the cell. Unlike cytotoxic T-cells, NK cells are not primed to attack specific target cells, and how they recognize their targets is unclear.

Natural selection. A mechanism of evolution in which different phenotypes have different survival and reproductive rates due to differing responses of the phenotypes to the environment. If phenotypic differences are at least partially genetically determined then natural selection can lead to evolution.

a. Observation: populations typically have the potential to grow faster than resources available to them.

b. Inference: Individuals of the population will end up competing for resources.

c. Observation: Individuals in a population vary in terms ofphenotype.

d. Observation: The phenotype is typically at least partially heritable.

e. Observation: Individuals vary, based on their phenotype in their ability to survive and leave offspring.

f. Inference: gene frequencies will change over time in response to the environment

g. Inference: Therefore the phenotypes found in the population will change over time.

Nauplius. An early free-swimming larval stage of some crustaceans. It possesses only three pairs of appendages and later molts to form the cypris larva. The nauplius is important in the life cycle of the barnacle as it is the stage during which this sessile animal is dispersed.

Neanderthal man. A species of early man, Homo neanderthalensis, that lived in Europe from about 150000 years ago and was replaced by modern man, H.sapiens, about 30000 years ago. They were dominant in western Europe during the first stages of the last glaciation, were cavedwelling, and made regular use of fire and tools.

Nearctic. One of the six zoogeographical regions, including North America from the Central Mexican Plateau in the south to the Aleutian Islands and Greenland in the north. The fauna include mountain goat, pronghorn antelope, caribou, and muskrat.

Nectar. A sugar-containing fluid secreted by the nectaries in plants.

Nectary A patch of glandular epidermal cells on the receptacle or other parts ofcertain flowers, producing a sugary liquid than attracts insects. The epidermal, and sometimes underlying, cells of the nectary may or may not be organized into clearly defined structures. Nectaries are an adaptation to encourage cross-pollination by insects.

Negative staining. A method of preparation of material for electron microscopy used for studying three-dimensional and surface features, notably of viruses, macromolecules, and the cristae of mitochondria. A stain is used that covers the background and penetrates surface features of the specimen, but leaves the specimen itself unstained.

Nekton. Animals of the pelagic zone of a sea or lake that are free-swimming and independent of tides, currents, and waves, such as fish, whales, squid, crabs, and shrimps. Nekton are limited in distribution by temperature and nutrient supply, and decrease with increasing depth.

Neolithic. The recent Stone Age, dating from about 10000 years ago until the beginning of the Bronze Age. It is characterized by more advanced and often polished some tools and the development of agriculture.

Neopallium A type of nerve tissue that constitutes most of the cerebral cortex of mammalian brains. It consists of several layers of nerve cell bodies with a highly complex network of connecting fibres and it is the most advanced type of cerebral cortical tissue in vertebrates.

Neoteny The retention of larval or other juvenile features beyond the normal stage in the development of an animal. It may be either temporary, because of climatic or other factor, or permanent, in which case the animal breeds in the larval stage. Neoteny is thought to be important in the evolution of some groups, including humans, who have certain resemblances to young stages of apes.

Neotropical Oe of the six main zoogeographical regions of the earth. It includes South and Central America, the West Indies, and the Mexican lowlands. The characteristic fauna includes sloths, armadillos, anteaters, cavies, vampire bats, llama, aplaca, peccary, rhea, toucan, curassows, and certain hummingbirds.

Nephridium. A simple excretory system found in many invertebrates which often relies on diffusion combined with current flow set up be a series of ciliated cells called flame cells.

Nephron. The basic unit of the vertebrate kidney. The nephron in mammals consists of **Bowman's capsule**, the **distal convoluted tubule**, the **Loop of Henle** and the **proximal convoluted tubule**.

Nereis. A genus of polychaete worms, the ragworms, found in the intertidal zone, where at low tide they form U-shaped burrows in the mud. Nereis can swim and crawl by using the segmentally arranged limblike parapodia. Nereis is carnivorous, seizng prey with its toothed pharynx.

Neritic. The marine environment from low water level to a depth of about 200 m, a zone that in many areas corresponds to the extent of the continental shelf. It makes up less than 1% of the marine environment. Nutrients are relatively abundant in this zone and it is penetrated by sunlight.

Nerve. A bundle of nerve fibers, surrounded by a protective covering of connective tissue. Mixed nerves, such as the spinal nerves, contain both sensory and motor fibres.

Nerve cord. An enclosed cylindrical tract of nerve fibres that forms a central route for the conduction of nerve impulses within the body. Vertebrates and other chordates have a single hollow nerve cord situated dorsally. Invertebrates generally have two or more nerve cords, each lacking a central cavity and with ganglia situated at intervals along its length.

Nerve net. A netlike layer of interconnecting nerve cells that is found in the body wall of certain groups of invertebrate animals; the most primitive type of nervous system. It occurs in cnidarians, echinoderms, and hemichordates.

Neural arch. An arch of bone or cartilage that arises dorsally from the centrum of a vertebra and encloses a canal-the spinal or neural canal-through which runs the spinal cord. It may bear a number of projections, such as a neural spine, for attachment of muscles.

Neutral mutations. Mutations are called neutral if they have no obvious effect on an organism's survival and reproductive success. They are important because neutral mutations may accumulate in a population through time and provide a source of variation for natural selection to act on should the environment change.

Neural plate. A strip of ectoderm, above the notochord, that lies along the central axis of the early embryos of chordates and develops into the central nervous system. The neural plate folds and forms the neural tube; this process is called neurulation. During the stage when the neural tube is forming the embryo is known as a neurula.

Neural tube. A hollow tube of tissue in the early embryo ofvertebrates that subsequently develops into the brain and spinal cord. It forms by folding of the ectodermal neural plate and has a central canal running through it. Sometimes the folds of the neural plate fail to close properly, resulting in neural tube defects in the fetus.

Neurite. Any projection from the cell body of a neuron, especially an immature neuron. As the neuron develops, neutrites can become either dendrites or axons.

Neurofibril. Any of the fibres in the cytoplasm of a nerve axon. Neurofibrils include neurofilaments and neurotubules, microtubules that play a role in the transport of proteins and other substances within the cytoplasm.

Neurofilament. A type of intermediate filament found in the axons of nerve cells. Neurofilaments serve as elements of the cytoskeleton supporting the axon cytoplasm.

Neurohaemal organ. A discrete body formed by a cluster of neurosecretory-cell terminals, where neurohormones are released into an adjacent blood space or capillary bed. Neurohaemal organs are found widely in both invertebrates and vertebrates.

Neurophysin. Either of two cysteine-rich proteins that bind to oxytocin and antidiuretic hormone in the neurohypophysis of the pituitary and are secreted with them. They have no hormonal activity and are cleaved from their respective hormones following secretion.

Neutron. A neutron is a negatively charged particle in the nucleus of an atom. Two atoms of the same element can have different numbers of neutrons and hence are called isotopes of each other.

Neurula. In chordates, an embryonic stage after gastrulation that is characterized by a dorsal infolding of the ectoderm. This infolding develops into the nervous system and the hollow dorsal nerve cord characteristic of **chordates**.

Neuston. The organisms that colonize the surface of an aquatic habitat. They are most abundant in freshwater habitats and include pond skaters, certain types of water beetles, and floating plants.

Neuter. An organisms that does not possess either male or female reproductive organs. Cultivated ornamental flowers that have neither pistils nor stamens are called neuters.

Neutral. Describing a compound or solution that is neither acidic nor basic. A neutral solution is one that contains equal numbers of both protonated and deprotonated forms of the solvent.

Neutrophil. A type of white blood cell that has a lobed nucleus and granular cytoplasm. Neutrophils egulf bacteria and release various substances, such as lysozyme and oxidizing agents.

Nicatinamide adenine dinucleotide(NAD+). An important electron and hydrogen ion acceptor in cellular respiration. This compound accepts electrons and transports them to electron transport systems involved in the production of ATP.

Nicatinamide adenine dinucleotide phosphate (NADP+). An important electron and hydrogen ion acceptor involved in transporting electrons used in biosynthetic pathways, for instance in the Calvin Benson cycle of photosynthesis.

Nictitating membrane. A clear membrane forming a third eyelid in amphibians, reptiles, birds, and some mammals. It can be drawn across the cornea independently of the other eyelids, thus clearing the eye surface and giving added protection without interrupting the continuity of vision.

Nitrogen. Symbol N. A colourless gaseous element that occurs in air and is an essential constituent of proteins and nuclei acids in living organisms.

Nitrogenous base. A basic compound containing nitrogen. The term is used especially of organic ring compounds, such as adenine, guanine, cytosine, and thymine, which are constituents of nucleic acids.

Nitrogenous waste. Any metabolic waste product that contains nitrogen. Urea and uric acid are the most common nitrogenous waste products in terrestrial animals; freshwater fish excrete ammonia and marine fish excrete both urea and trimethylamine oxide.

Node. For plants, the area of the stem where the leaves arise.

Nomad. A cell that migrates or wanders from its site of formation. Certain types of phagocytes are nomads.

Nondisjunction. The failure of homologous chromosomes to separate properly during meiosis resulting in a gamete with an excess or lack of one or more chromosomes. Disorders caused by nondisjunction include Down's syndrome in humans.

Nonreducing sugar. A sugar that cannot donate electrons to other molecules and therefore cannot act as a reducing agent. Sucrose is the most common nonreducing sugar. The linkage between the glucose and fructose units in sucrose, which inolves aldehyde and ketone groups, is responsible for the inability of sucrose to act as a reducing sugar.

Nonsense mutation. A type of point mutation that converts a codon normally specifying an amino acid to one of the stop codons, thus signalling termination of translation and causing synthesis of the polypeptide chain to cease prematurely.

Nose. The protuberance on the face of some vertebrates that contains the nostrils and part of the nasal cavity. It therefore forms part of the olfactory system and the external opening of the respiratory system.

Nucellus. The tissue that makes up the greater part of the ovule of seed plants. It contains the embryo sac and nutritive tissue. It is enclosed by the integuments except for a small gap, the micropyle. In certain flowering plants it may persist after fertilization and provide nutrients for the embryo.

Nuclear-cytoplasmic ratio. A measure of the size of a cell nucleus in relation to the cytoplasm. The nuclear-cytoplasmic ratio is often used as an index in the comparison of cells from normal and abnormal tissues. For example, cultured cancer cells show an increase in the nuclear-cytoplasmic ratio.

Nuclease. Any enzyme that breaks down nucleic acids to nucleotides. Nucleases are found in the small intestine.

Nucleic acid. Any one of several polymers of nucleotides. **Deoxyribonucleic acid**(RNA) is the nucleic acid found in the chromosomes and that we know makes up the genetic material of organisms and many viruses. The DNA nitrogen bearing bases are adenine, guanine, cytosine and thymine and the sugar is deoxyribose. The various **ribonucleic acids(RNA)** are nucleic acids that serve a number of functions related to protein synthesis and for some viruses serve as the genetic material. Unlike DNA, the RNA's contain uracil instead of thymine and use the sugar ribose.

Nucleoid. The part of a cell of a bacterium that contains the genetic material DNA and therefore controls the activity of the cell. It corresponds to the nucleus of the more advanced eukaryotic cells but is not bounded by a membrane.

Nucleotidase. An enzyme that catalyses the breakdown of nucleotides. It is present in the epithelial cells of the small linestine and plays an important role in the digestion of proteins.

Nucleotide. In biochemistry, a molecule consisting of a phosphate group and a one or two ring nitrogen containing base, both of which are attached to a five carbon sugar. The five carbon sugar may be either ribose or deoxyribose depending on the nucleotide.

Nucleolus. A dark circular region inside the nucleus during interphase. This region consists of areas of duplicated DNA for rapid RNA transcription related to the production of ribosomal RNA.

Nucleoplasm. The material contained within the nucleus of a cell. The nucleoplasm is bound by the nuclear envelope, which separates it from the cytoplasm.

Nucleoside. An organic compound consisting of a nitrogen-containing purine or pyrimidine base linked to a sugar. An example is adenosine.

Nucleosome. The basing level of coiling in a eukaryote chromosome, consisting of a large histone protein wrapped by several coils of DNA with the coils head in place by a smaller assembly of histone proteins.

Nucleus. An organelle in all eukaryotic cells that contains the bulk of the cell's DNA. The nucleus is surrounded by a double membrane envelope perforated with protein lined pores for the entrance and egress of large molecules.

Nutation. The spiral movement of a plant organ during growth, also known as circumnutation. It is seen in climbing plants and helps the plant find a suitable support to twine around. Examples are the coiling movements of the shoot tips of runner beans and of the tendrils of sweet peas.

Nutrition. The process by which organisms obtain energy for growth, maintenance, and repair. There are two main types of nutrition: heterotrophic nutrition. employed by animals, fungi, and certain bacteria; and autotrophic nutrition, found in most plants and bacteria.

Nymph. The juvenile stage of exopterygote insects, especially terrestrial species, such as grasshoppers, cockroaches, and earwigs; the juveniles of aquatic species. are sometimes called naiads or larvae. The lymph resembles the adult except that the wings and reproductive organs are undeveloped. There is no pupal stage, the nymph developing directly into the adult.

O

Objective. The lens or system of lenses nearest to the object being examined through an optical instrument.

Obligate. Required. For example obligate aerobes are

organisms that require oxygen to grow. Obligate anaerobes require the absence of oxygen to grow. Contrast **facultative** which means can use but not required.

Obligate anaerobes. Organisms that cannot use free oxygen for respiration. Oxygen may inhibit the growth of obligate anaerobes or kill them.

Oceanic zone. The region of the open sea beyond the edge of the continental shelf, where the depth is greater than 200 metres.

Ocellus. A simple eye occurring in insects and other invertebrates. It typically consists of light-sensitive cells and a single cuticular lens.

Odontoblast. A cell that is responsible for producing the dentine of vertebrate teeth. Odontoblasts are found around the lining of the pulp cavity and have processes that extend into the dentine.

Odorant. A substance that is responsible for the perception of a smell and is thus detected by olfactory organs, such as the nose.

Oesophagus. The section of the alimentary canal that lies between the pharynx and the stomach. It is a muscular tube whose function is to transfer food to the stomach by means of wavelike contractions along its length.

Offspring. New individual organisms that result from the process of sexual or asexual reproduction.

Oil. Any of various viscous liquids that are generally immiscible with water. Natural plant and animal oils are either volatile mixtures of terpenes and simple esters or are glycerides of fatty acids.

Oleaginous. Producing or containing oil or lipids. Oleaginous microorganisms, which normally contain 20-25% oil, are of interest in biotechnology as alternative sources of lipids or as possible sources for novel oils. The majority of the oils produced by oleaginous eukaryotic microorganisms are similar to plant oils.

Olecranon process. A bony process on the ulna in the forelimb or vertebrates that projects beyond the joint between the humerus and the ulna.

Olfaction. The sense of smell or the process of detecting smells. This is achieved by receptors in olfactory organs that are sensitive to air-or water-borne chemicals. Stimulation of these receptors results in the transmission of information to the brain via the olfactory nerve.

Olfactory lobe. Either member of a pair of lobes in the forebrain, at the anterior end of the cerebrum. They contain the endings of the olfactory nerves and are concerned with the sense of smell, being prominent in the dogfish and other animals that depend on this sense.

Oligocene. The third geological epoch of the Palaeogene period. It began about 34 million years ago, following the Eocene epoch, and extended for about 11 million years to the beginning of the Miocene epoch. The epoch was characterized by the continued rise of mammals; the first pigs, rhinoceroses, and tapirs made their appearance.

Oligochaeta. A class of hermaphrodite annelid worms that bear only a few bristles. Oligochaetes are very abundant in freshwater and terrestrial habitats. The most familiar members of the class are the earthworm and the freshwater bloodworm.

Oligotrophic. Describing a body of water with a poor supply of nutrients and a low rate of formation of organic matter by photosynthesis.

Omasum. The third of four chambers that form the stomach of ruminants.

Oncogene. A gene that when defective is known to cause cancer.

Ommatidium(a). The basic unit of the arthropod compound eye. An arthropod eye can consist of thousands of ommatidia.

Omnivore. An animal that eats both animal and vegetable matter. Pigs, for example, are omnivorous.

Omnivorous. Literally eating all; eating a wide variety of foodstuff. Humans are the ultimate omnivores.

Ontogeny. The Developmental course of an organism from the fertilized egg through to maturity. It has been suggested that ontogeny recapitulates 'phylogeny', i.e.

the stages of development, especially of the embryo, reflect the evolutionary history of the organism. This idea is now discredited.

Oogamy. Sexual reproduction involving the formation and subsequent fusion of a large, usually stationary, female gamete and a small motile male gamete. The female gamete may contain nourishment for the development of the embryo, which is often retained and protected by the parent organisms.

Oogonium. 1. The female sex organ of algae and fungi. 2. Any of the immature sex cells in the animal ovary that give rise to oocytes by mitotic divisions.

Oospore. A zygote that is produed as a result of oogamy in certain algae and fungi. It contains food reserves, develops a protective outer covering, and enters a resting phase before germination.

Open circulatory system. A circulatory system where the "blood" is carried part of the time in large vessels but spends some of the time bathing the organs directly rather than flowing through capillaries as would be the case in a **closed circulatory system**.

Operon. A region of DNA which includes a promotor, operator and structural genes. The **promotor** is a site for attachment of RNA polymerase, the **operator** a site for repressor protein attachment, and the **structural genes** can be transcribed by the **RNA polymerase** if it can travel from the promotor to those genes for transcription.

Opiate. One of a group of drugs derived from opium, an extract of the poppy plant Papaver somniferum that depresses brain function. Opiates include morphine and its synthetic derivatives, such as heroin and codeine. They are used in medicine chiefly to relieve pain, but the use of morphine and heroin is strictly controlled since they an cause drug dependence and tolerance.

Opioid. Any one of a group of substances that bind to opioid receptors to produce pharmacological and physiological effects similar to those of morphine. Opiods are not necessarily structurally similar to morphine, although a subgroup of opioids, the opiates, are morphine derived compounds. The endogenous opioids, which occur naturally in the body, comprise the endorphins, enkephalins and dynorphins.

Opioid receptor. Any cell receptor molecule that binds an morphine or an endogenous opioid.

Opisthosoma. The posterior section of the body of arachnids and other arthropods of the phylum Chelicerata, which consists of those body segments that do not bear legs.

Opportunistic. Describing a species that can quickly exploit new resources as they arise, for example by rapidly colonizing a new environment. Such species characteristically exhibit.

Opsin. The lipoprotein component of rhodopsin, the light-sensitive pigment that occurs in the rod cells of the retina.

Opsonization. The process in which certain antibodies in the blood bind to the surface of an invading microorganisms, which renders it more susceptible to phagocytosis by macrophages and neutrophils. Acutephase response proteins also act as opsonins, as do complemet proteins.

Optical rotation. Rotation of the plane of polarization of plane-polarized light by an optically active substance.

Optic chiasma. The site in the floor of the vertebrate forebrain at which fibres entering via the optic nerves cross to the opposite side of the brain, forming an X-shaped pattern. In humans and other mammals with good stereoscopic vision, only half the fibres from each side cross over. In lower vertebrates, nearly all the fibres may cross over.

Optic nerve. The second cranial nerve; a paired sensory nerve that runs from each eye to the brain. It is responsible for conveying visual stimuli received by the rods and cones in the retina to the brain for interpretation.

Optic vesicle. The outgrowth from the forebrain of a vertebrate embryo that develops into the retina of the eye. When the optic vesicle comes into contact with the ectoderm covering the head of the embryo, these ectodermal cells become thicker: the ectoderm in this region invaginates and eventually becomes detached from the adjacent ectodermal cells to form the lens of the eye.

Optimum. The value of some variable or set of variables at which some process works best at. Enzymes in our bodies for example have their maximum catalytic ability at a temperature of 37°C. So we also say that the the optimum temperature for these enzymes to function is at 37°C.

Orbit. One of two cavities or depressions in the vertebrate skull that contain the eyeballs and their associated muscles, blood vessels, nerves, etc.

Orbital. An orbital is the shape of the probability clouds that electrons are found in at a certain energy level or shell. The way the electrons are added to a shell and its orbitals is determined by rules based on quantum mechanics. For example, each orbital can hold at most two electrons.

Order. A collection of similar families. Plant orders generaly end in ales but animal orders do not have any particular ending. Orders may be divided into suborders. Similar orders constitute a class.

Ordovician. The second oldest period of the Paleozoic era, some 510-440 million years ago. It is characterized by an abundance of marine invertebrates but an almost total absence of vertebrates apart from some jawless fish. Many of the invertebrates were primitive forms of life that have no living representatives.

Organ. A body structure composed of two or more tissues.

Organ culture. The maintenance or growth of living organs, usually embryonice, in vitro. In animals the organ must be small to enable diffusion of nutrients and excretory products to and from the inner cells and is thus usually embryonic. Mature plant organs, notably roots, may be cultured indefinitely in suitable media.

Organelle. A distinct and large scale structure within a cell for carrying out a particular set of functions. Organelles are often surrounded by one or more plasma membranes and sometimes the definition is restricted to just such structures. We term such organelles "**membrane bound organelles**."

Organic compound. A compound consisting of carbon, hydrogen and often oxygen and other elements. The term originally arose because scientists thought only living things could make organic compounds. We know that organic compounds can be made from non-living chemicals. It should be noted that artificially made organic compounds are not better or worse than those from living things.

Oriental. One of the six zoogeographical regions of the earth. It includes the Southern Asian countries of India, Southeast Asia, and the western Malay archipelago. The characteristic fauna include the Indian elephant, rhinoceros, macaque, gibbon, orangutan, jungle fowl, and peacock. The boundary between this region and the Australasian region has been the subject of contention in the past.

Origin of life. Geological evidence strongly suggests that life originated on earth about 4000 million years ago. The basic components of organic matter water, methane, ammonia, and related compounds-were abundant in the atmosphere. Energy from the sun and lightning storms caused these to recombine into increasingly complex organic molecules. Particular combinations of such complex substances eventually showed the characteristics of living organisms.

Ornithiscia. Extinct order of ARCHOSAURS, lasting throughout Jurassic to late Cretaceous. 'Bird-hipped'and herbivorous dinosaurs. Some early forms were bipedal. Both the pubes and ischia of the PELVIC GIRDLE pointed downwards and backwards. Included stegosaurs, ankylosaurs and ceratopsids.

Ornithology. The branch of vertebrate zoology that is

concerned with the study of birds.

Orphan receptors. Receptors for which no ligand has yet been found. For orphan nuclear receptor superfamily.

Orthogenesis. An early theory of evolution in which evolutionary change was envisaged as occurring in a definite direction and along a predetermined route, irrespective of natural selection. Orthogenesis therefore conflicts with conventional evolutionary theory such as neo-Darwinism.

Orthognathous. 'Short-faced' mammals, lacking muzzles. Hominid evolution has been accompanied by the evolution of increasingly orthognathous faces from PROGNATHOUS ones.

Orthotropous. Describing the position of the ovule in the ovary, in which the ovule has developed vertically so that the micropylar and is directly over the funicle as in Polygonum.

Osculum. Large opening through which water leaves the body of a sponge having entered through ostia.

Osmium tetraoxide. Substance which, in aqueous solution, blackens fat and is often used to demonstrate myelin sheaths of neurons. Used as a fixative in light and electron microscopy.

Osmophilic body. Lipid-containing granules, appearing dark when treated with osmium fixation.

Osmoregulation. The ability of organisms to control the concentration of water and solutes in their bodily fluids. Many marine organisms for instance cannot do this since they spend their whole lives at one osmotic concentration. Such organisms are called osmoconformers. Other organisms that spend their lives on land or in fresh and salt water can regulate their internal osmotic concentration. These are called osmoregulators.

Osmosis. The diffusion of water (or some other solvent) across a semipermeable (selectively permeable) membrane.

Osmotic pressure. The pressure that would have to be inserted on the hypertonic side of a selectively permeable membrane to prevent a net flow of water across the membrane from the hypotonic side. This is a measure of a solution's ability to take on water. A really important concept in understanding fluid flow in plants...bcause after all, neither plants nor scarecrows have hearts to circulate fluids.

Osmotroph. Any heterotrophic organism that btains its nutrients by absorbing organic matter in solution from its surroundings.

Ossicle. Any small bony or chitinous structure found in various skeletal parts of animals. The term ossicle usually refers to any of the chain of bones in the mammalian ear.

Osteoblast. Cell type responsible for formation of calcified intercellular matrix of BONE.

Osteoclast. Multinucleate cell which breaks down the calcified intercellular matrix of BONE. Remodelling of bone shape by such activity accompanies boe GROWTH.

Osteostraci. Extinct order of AGNATHA. Head covered by strog bony shield. Heterocercal tail.

Ostiole. Pore in fruit bodies of certain fungi, and in conceptacles of brown algae through which, respectively, spores or gametes are discharged.

Ostium. 1. One of the many inhalant pores of sponges. 2. Opening in the arthropod heart, into which blood flows from the haemocole.

Otolith. A gelatinous mass containing a high concentration of particles of calcium carbonate, which forms part of the macula of the inner ear.

Outer ear. The part of the ear external to the tympanum. It is preset in mammals, birds, and some reptiles and consists of a tube that directs sound waves onto the tympanum. In mammals it may include an external pinna, which extends beyond he skull.

Overpopulation. The situation that arises when rapid growth of a population, usually a human population, results in numbers that canot be supported by the available resources, such as space and food. This occurs when the birth rate food. This occurs when the birth rate exceeds the death rate, or when immagination exceeds emigration, or when a combination of these factors exists.

Oviduct. The tube that conveys an animal egg cell from the ovary to other parts of the reproductive system or to the outside. Eggs are passed along the oviduct by the action of muscles and cilia.

Oviparity. Reproduction in which fertilized eggs are laid or spawned by the mother and batch outside her body. It occurs in most animals except marsupial and placental mammals.

Ovipositor. An organ at the hind end of the abdomen of female insects through which eggs are laid. It consists of a pair of modified appendages and is often long and piercing, so that eggs can be laid in otherwise inaccessible places. The sting of bees and wasps is a modified ovipositor.

Ovoviviparity. Reproduction in which fertilized eggs develop and hatch in the oviduct of the mother. It occurs in many invertebrates and in some fish and reptiles.

Ovulation. The release of an egg cell from the ovary, which in mammals in stimulated by luteinizing hormoe. The developing egg cell within its follicle migrates to the oary surface, when mature, it is released from the follicle into the body cavity, from where it passes into the oviduct.

Ovule. An plants, the structure found in the carpels at the base of the flower that develops into the seed.

Ovuliferous scale. One of a group of large woody specialized leaves that form the female cone of conifers and related trees. It bears the ovules, which develop into seeds.

Ovum (egg cell). 1. The mature reproductive cell of female animals, which is produced by the ovary. It is spherical, has a nucleus, is covered with an egg membrane, and is not mobile. 2. The oosphere of plants.

Oxalic acid. A crystalline solid, that is slightly soluble in water. Oxalic acid is strongly acidic and very poisonous. It occurs in certain plants, e.g. sorrel and the leaf blades of rhubarb.

Oxaloacetate(Oxaloacetic acid). An organic acid with four carbons that is the starting material for the Kreb's citric acid cycle. Its function is to pick up two energy rich carbons from other parts of metabolism feeding into the Kreb's cycle.

Oxidase. Any enzyme that catalyses oxidation-reduction reactions that involve the transfer of electrons to molecular oxygen.

Oxidation. The process by which electrons are removed from a chemical. The chemical is then said to be oxidized while whatever chemical receives the electrons is said to be reduced.

Oxidative deamination. A reaction involved in the catabolism of amino acids that assists their excretion from the body.

Oxidative decarboxylation. The reaction in the Krebs cycle in which oxygen, derived from two water molecules, is used to oxidize two carbon atoms to two carbon atoms result from the decarboxylation reactions that occur during the Krebs cycle as the six-carbon compound citrate is converted to the four-carbon compound oxaloacetate.

Oxidoreductase. Any of a class of enzymes that catalyse oxidation reduction reactions, i.e. they are involved in the transfer of hydrogen or electrons between molecules. They include the oxidases and dehydrogenases.

Oxygen. An element with eight protons and eight electrons and with an atomic mass averaging a bit over 16. Oxygen is important because of its strong tendency to grab electrons. Under current conditions, oxygen is a waste product of photosynthesis. In aerobic cellular respiration, oxygen is the final electron Acceptor from the electron transport systems.

P

Parapatric speciation. Parapatric speciation is speciation involving geographical isolation and divergence of two or more populations from a parent species. The speciation process is completed with the evolution of species isolating mechanisms which prevent mistaken interbreeding. Parapatric speciation is different than allopatric speciation in that the completion of speciation involves the evolution of post zygotic species isolating mechanisms. However the distinction between allopatric and parapatric speciation isn't always clear.

Pachytene. In meiosis, the stage in midprophase I that is characterized by the contraction of paired homologous chromosomes. At this point each chromosome consists of a pair of chromatids and the two associated chromosomes are termed a tetrad.

Paedogenesis. Reproduction in the larval or other juvenile stage by animals exhibiting permanent neoteny. For example, the axolotlthe larva of a salamanderis able to produce off spring similar to itself.

Palearctic. One of the six zoogeographical regions, including Europe, the USSR, northern Arabia, and the Mediterranean coastal strip of Africa. The fauna include the hedgehog, wild boar, and fallow and roe deer.

Paleocene. The oldest epoch of the teritary, 65-55 million years ago, represented in Britain by marine sand deposits at Thanet. It is characterized by the absence of dinosaurs and the presence of various primitive mammals, now extinct. The first insectivores, rodents, and primates are also found.

Paleoecology. The investigation of prehistoric ecology as revealed by studying fossils and their artefacts, pollen samples and the mineral deposits in which such structures occur.

Paleolithic. The older Stone Age, when stone tools can first be recognized as such, extending from about 2 million years ago to about 10000 years ago.

Paleontology. The study of extinct organisms, including their fossil remains, and impressions left by them, Sometimes the subject is divided into palebotany, the study of fossil plants, and paleozoology, the study of fossil animals.

Paleozoic. The first and oldest era in which life became abundant, about 590-230 million years ago. It is divided into six main periods; the Cambrian Ordovician, Silurian, Devonian, Carboniferous, and Permian. Beginning with aquatic invertebrates and algae, the era ended with the invasion of land by tree ferns and reptiles.

Palmella. A stage formed under certain conditions in various unicellular algae in which, after division, the daughter cells remain within the envelope of the parent cell and are thus rendered immobile. The cells may continue dividing giving a multicellular mass, which is contained in a gelatinous matrix. Palmellod forms may develop undulipodia and revert to normal molile cells at any time. Members of the algal genus Palmella typically exist in the palmella condition.

Palmitic acid. A saturated fatty acid occurring widely in fats and oils of animal and vegetable origin.

Pancreas. A gland lying between the spleen and the duodenum, and having a duct that enters the duodenum. It secretes pancreatic juice which contains various enzymes, including; trypsin for breaking down proteins to amino acids, amylase for converting starch to maltose, and lipase for changing emulsified oils to glycerin and fatty acids. The gland also contains endocrine tissues and produces insulin and glucagon.

Pangenesis. The theory, no longer accepted, introduced by Darwin to explain the inheritance of variation. He postulated that the body fluids carry particles from all over the body to the reproductive cells where they affect the hereditary material and thus the characters inherited by the next generation. Pangenesis was used to explain the erroneous theory of the inheritance of acquired characteristics.

Panicle. A compound raceme formed by branching of the peduncle, each branch bearing a raceme, e.g. oat. The term is often applied to any sort of branched racemose inflorescence, for example the horse chestnut, in which each branch is actually a cyme.

Pantothenic acid. One of the watersoluble B-group of vitamins. Sources of the vitamin include egg yolk, kidney, liver and yeast. As a constituent of coenzyme A, pantothenic acid is essential for several fundamental reactions in metabolism. A deficiency results in symptoms affecting a wide range if tissues; the oer all effects include fatigue, poor motor coordination, and muscle cramps.

Papilla. 1. A short sometimes coneshaped hair often found on petals and giving them their velvety appearance. It is a extension of the outer wall of the epidermal cell.

2. A small nipple-like projection from a surface of an animal tissue or organ.

Papovavirus. One of a group of small DNA-containing viruses,about 50 nm in diameter, that cause tumors in animals. The group includes SV40, a much-studied virus originally isolated from the African green monkey and belonging to a subgroup called the polyomaviruses.

Pappus. The ring of hairs, scales, or teeth that makes up the calyx in flowers of the Compositae. It persists on the fruit and serves to aid the wind dispersal of seeds. An example is the cypsela of the dandelion in which the pappus remains attached by a long thin stalk and acts as a parachute.

Parabiosis. The experimental or natural union of two similar animals so that their blood circulations are continuous. Experimental parabiosis is often performed on insects to study what effects chemicals in one individual have when passed to the other. Natural parabiosis occurs in Siamese twins.

Parallel evolution. The development of similar features in closely related organisms as a result of strong selection in the same direction. There are few examples of this phenomenon.

Paraphysis. A sterile unbranched multicellular hair found in large numbers between the reproductive organs of certain algae Club-shaped hyphae in the hymenial layer of certain basidiomycete fungi are also termed paraphyses, and similar structures are also found in the ascocarps of ascomycete fungi.

Parapodium. A lobed lateral appendage, pairs of which occur on all segments of a polychaete worm except the first two and the last one. Parapodia act as paddles for swimming and provide a large respiratory surface. The surface of the parapodium is well supplied with blood capillaries to increase the rate of exchange of respiratory gases.

Parasitism. A type of symbiosis where one partner benefits and the other one is harmed.

Paratonic movements. Movements of plants in response to external stimuli. They may be divided into mechanical movements (e.g. the hygroscopic movements of dead cells) and movements caused by the stimulation of sensitive cells.

Parazoa. A subkingdom of the kingdom Animalia containing the phylum Porifera. In some recent classifications it also contains the phylum Placozoa, comprising the tiny marine organism Trichoplax.

Parietal eye. A third eye that develops from an anterior outgrowth of the forebrain of early vertebrates.

Parthenocarpy The development of fruit in unfertilized flowers, resulting in seedless fruits. It may occur naturally, as in the banana. It may also be induced artificially by the application of auxin, as in commercial tomato growing.

Passive cells. Endodermal cells that have Casparian strips but remain otherwise unthickened after deposits of lignin and cellulose have been laid down elsewhere in the endodermis. Passage cells are found opposite the protoxylem and allow transport of water and solutes from the cortex to the stele. They are particularly common in the endodermis of older monocotyledon roots.

Passerines. Birds in which the feet are adapted for grasping branches, having three toes pointing forwards and one pointing backwards. They constitute the largest order of birds, with over 5000 species, and include the larks, thrushes, warblers, finches, sparrows, and starlings.

Passive immunity. A type of apparent resistance to a foreign antigen obtained by injecting the patient with an appropriate set of antibodies produced by another organism. Passive immunity is temporary and used in situations when the patient's own immune system could not mount a defense in time to save the individual.

Passive transport. The passage of substances through a plasma membrane without the use of cellular energy.

Pasteurization. The partial sterilization of foodstuffs by heating to a temperature below boiling. This kills harmful microorganisms but retains the flavor. It is named after the pionner of the method, Louis Pasteur, who used it to prevent apolage of wine and beer.

Patella. The small bone in front of the knee joint between the femur and tibia of the hind limb of most mammals, some birds, and some reptiles, it forms the kneecap in humans. It is a sesamoid bone., having developed in the tendon of the quadriceps femoris muscle.

Pathogen. A pathogen is a disease causing organism or virus. In addition to viruses, some bacteria and protista are important pathogens as are certain fungi and animals.

Peat. Accumulated dead plant material which has remained incompletely decomposed owing, principally, to lack of oxygen. Occurs in moorland, bogs and fens, where land is more or less completely waterlogged; often forms a layer several metres deep. Of local value as fuel for burning.

Pectic compounds. Acid polysaccharide carbohydrates, present in CELL WALLS of unlignified plant tissues; comprise pectic acid and pectates, pectose and pectin. Form gels under certain conditions Principal components are galacturonic acid, galactose, arabinose and methanol. Form the basis of fruit jellies.

Pedicel. Stalk of individual flower of an inflorescence. Narrow tube-like 'waist' of many hymenopteran insects.

Pedipalps. Second pair of head appendages of ARACHNIDA.

Peduncle. 1. Stalk of an inflorescence. 2. An extensible pseudopod used to catch and either suck out or engulf a prey organism found in some members of the DINOPHYTA.

Peking man. Early form of Homo erectus from China; formerly termed Sinanthropus.

Pelagic. Inhabiting the mass of water of lake or sea bottom. Pelagic animals and plants are divided into PLANKTON and NEKTON.

Pellicle. An outer skin-like layer comprising mostly protein found around cells of some unicellular algae. In the DINOPHYTA it is an additional wall layer or envelope made of cellulose and sporopopollenin-like material, lying below the theca.

Peltate. Circular, with the stak inserted in the middle, as of some leaves, hairs and horsetail and cycad sporangiophores.

Pelvis. 1. The PELVIC GIRDLE. 2. Lower part of the vertebrate abdomen, bounded by the pelvic girdle. 3. The renal pelvis.

Penis. Unpaired intromittant organ of male mammals, some reptiles and a few birds. In mammals, contains the terminal part of the urethra.

Pentadactyl limb. The type of limb found in tetrapod vertebrates. Evolved as an adaptation to terrestrial lifefrom the paired fins of crossopterygian fishes. The basic plan is illustrated in Fig. 132. Many modifications occur through loss or fusion of elements, especially in the terminal parts. The earliest known tetrapods from the Upper Devonian, had more tha five digits, raising the possibility that the pentadactyl condition is not primitive for the clade.

Pentastomids. Phylum Pentastoma. Bilaterally symmetrical, flattened, pseudocoelomate and parasitic worms 90% of known species parasitize reptilesand all parasitize vertebrates. Separate sexes; fertilization internal. Development via three 'larval' stages, the first with three pairs of lobed, leg-like and unjointed apendages.

Pentosans. Polysaccharide whose monomers are PENTOSE units. Include many HEMICELLULOSES, although these more often contain non-pentose units as well.

Pentose. Monosaccharide with five-carbon atoms in molecule, e.g. ribose and deoxyribose and ribulose. Found in various plant polysaccharide chains, e.g. pectin, gum arabic.

Pepsin. An enzyme in the stomach that digests proteins down to the level of small polypeptides. Enzymes that break down peptide bonds are also called **Peptidases**.

Peptidase. One of a group of enzymes hydrolysing peptides into component amino acids. Also sometimes used of proteotytic enzymes in general.

Peptide bond. A bond between the amino end of one amino acid and the carboxyl end of the next amino acid. The term **peptide** is also used for a short chain of amino acids strung together by peptide bonds...while **polypeptide** is another term for protein.

Peptone. Large fragment produced by initial process of protein hydrolysis.

Permeable. Able to let other substances pass through. Used to describe a membrane. Contrast **semi-permeable**.

Permease. A protein that serves as a gateway or channel to allow diffusion of substances through a plasma membrane. May refer to a gated or ungated channel. This type of diffusion is called **faciliated diffusion**.

Perennation. (Of plants) surviving from year to year vegetative means.

Perennial. Plant that continuous its growth from year to year. In herbaceous parennials, the aerial parts die back in autumn and are replaced by new growth the following year from the underground structure. In woody perennials, permanent woody stems above ground form starting point for each year's growth, a characteristic enabling some species to attain large size.

Perforation plate. End wall of a vessel element containing one or more holes or performations.

Perforins. Proteins released from granules by cytotoxic T CELLS, disrupting the integrity of the target cell membrane by forming channels there, in the presence of calcium ions.

Pericardial cavity. Space enclosing the heart. In vertebrates, is coelomic and bounded by a double-walled sac, the pericardium. In arthropods and molluscs, is haemocoelic, supplying blood to heart.

Pericarp. Wall of an ovary after it has matured into a FRUIT. May be dry, membranous or hard, or fleshy.

Perichaetium. Distinct whorl of leaves surrounding sex organs in mosses.

Periclinal. (Bot) (Of planes of division of cells) running parallel to the surface of the plant.

Pericycle. Tissue of the vascular cylinder lying immediately within the ENDODERMIS, comprising parenchyma cells and sometimes fibres.

Periderm. Cork cambium and its products; i.e. cork and secondary cortex.

Perigene development. Development of GUARD CELLS in which the guard cell mother does not give rise to subsidiary cells.

Perigonium. The antheridium, together with associated perigonial leaves or bracts, borne on a specialized branch in mosses and liveworts.

Perikaryon. Alternative term for CELL BODY of neurone.

Perineum. Region between anus and urogenital openings of placental mammals.

Periosteum. Sheath of connective tissue investing vertebrate bones, and to which tendons attach.

Periplasmic space. Space between the two cell membrane of Gramnegative bacteria or an organelle envelope. Proteins with the correct signal sequence can be targeted to this region.

Periplastidial compartment. The narrow space between the chloroplast and the chloroplast endoplasmic reticulum in the HETEROKONTOPHYTA, CAYPTOPHYTA and CHLORARACHNIOPHYA.

Perisperm. Nutritive tissue surrounding the embryo in some seeds; derived from the NUCELLUS.

Peristalsis. Waves of contraction of smooth muscle, passing along tubular organs such as the intestines. Serve to move material from one end of the tube to the other.

Peristome. Fringe of pointed appendages around the opening of dehiscent moss capsule, concerned with spore liberation. Spirally twisted groove leading to cytostome in some ciliate protozoans.

Perithecium. Rounded, or flask-shaped, fruiting structure of some members of the ASCOMYCOTA and LICHENS; with an internal hymenium of asci and paraphyses, and opening via a pore through which ascospores are discharged.

Perivisceral cavity. The vertebrate coelomic cavity lined by PERITONEUM.

Permanent teeth. Second of the two successive sets of teeth of most mammals, replacing DECIDUOUS TEETH.

Permanent wilting point. The condition of a soil in which water is sufficiently unavailable to cause plants growing in it to wilt irrecoverably.

Permease. A TRANSPORT PROTEIN, or carrier, assisting in trnasport of a solute down its concentration gradient a cell membrane.

Peroxisome. A small organelle containing oxidative enzymes involved with the intracellular digestion of lipids and amino acids.

Perturbation approach. In community ecology, an experimental approach in which artificial disturbances are used to unravel species interactions.

Phaeophytin. A yellow-gray colored pigment of chlorophyll appearing in organic solvent extracts of chlorophyll and often seen during paper chromatography of such extracts.

Phagocyte. A cell that is capable of engulfing particles from its surroundings by a process termed phagocytosis. Examples are the neutrophils and macrophages in vertebrates, which play an important role in protecting the organism against infection.

Many other cells are capable of phagocytosis, e.g. intestinal epithelial cells and certain protoctists.

Phagocytosis. The active ingesting of solid particles, including other cells, by a cell.

Phalanges. Series of small rod-shaped bones that form the skeleton of the fingers and toes of tetrapod limbs. In the typical pentadactyl limbs of five digits, there are two phalanges in the first digit and three in each of the others. In some species they may be greatly elongated or reduced. They form hinge with each other ad with the metacarpals or metatarsals.

Phanerogam. In early classifications, any plant that reproduces by seed. The phanerogams are thus equivalent to the spermatophytes of more recent taxonomic systems.

Phanerophyte. A perennial plant with persistent shoots and buds well above soil level.

Phelloderm. The inner layer of the periderm.

Phenetic. Describing or relating to the observable similarities and differences between organisms. Phenetic classification systems are based on such characteristics, rather tha evolutionary relationship between groups.

Phenocopy. A change in the appearance of an organism caused by the environment, but which is similar in effet to a change caused by gene mutation. Such changes, which are not inherited, are generally caused by environmental factos affecting the organism at an early stage of development.

Phenolphthalein. An acid-alkali indicator that is colorless in acids and red in alkalis. It has a pH range from 8.4-10.0 and is a frequently used indicator for the detection of pH change in acid-alkali titrations. Phenolphthalien, together with borax, is used to test for saccharide derivatives, e.g. glycerol.

Phenotype. The observable characteristics of an organism, which are determined by the interaction of the genotype with the environment. Many genes present in the genotype do not show their effects in the phenotype because they are masked by dominant alleles. Genotypically identical orgaisms may have very different phenotypes in different environment, an effect particularly noticeable in plants grown in various habitats.

Phenylhydrazine. A colorless liquid that reacts aldehydes and ketones to give phenyl-hydrazones. These are white solids with definite melting points that can be used to identifty the respective aldehydes and ketones. With monosaccharides, phenylhydrazine forms osazones, yellow crystalline compounds, that are distinctive for most monosaccharides.

Phenylketonuria. A genetic disorder resulting in the inability to metabolize phenylalanine to tyrosine and causing severe mental retardation. Phenylketonuria is caused by a defective recessive gene and therefore both parents must be carriers for the child to be affected; it may be diagnosed by trhe presence of phenylpyruvic acid in the urine. If detected soon after birth, a diet low in phenylalanine will enable the infant to develop normally.

Phosphoglycerate(PGA). A three carbon intermediate important in the Calvin-Benson cycle in the part of the cycle leading to the production of PGAL.

Phosphoglyceraldehyde(PGAL). A three carbon compound found as an intermediate both in **glycolysis** and in the **Calvin-Benson cycle** of photosynthesis. Surplus PGAL harvested by the chloroplast is the true end product of the Calvin Benson cycle and in tern is used by the plant cell to produce fructose, then glucose and from there do all the other things that plants and the rest of the living world needs to do.

Phosphorylation. The process of adding a phosphate group to a molecule. The phosphate may be transferred from another organic molecule as in **substrate level phosphorylation** or be gotten as inorganic phosphate in the solution where the reaction is taking place as in **electron transport phosphorylation**. Phosphorylation is important in the production of ATP from ADP and phosphate.

Photic zone. The surface layer of an ocean

Photosynthesis. A two step process by which plants and other organisms take light energy, transfer it to electrons and use the electrons plus hydrogen ions to reduce carbon dioxide to produce sugars. In most modern forms of photosynthesis, oxygen is a waste product.

pH Scale. This scale is a logarithmic scale for expressing the concentration of hydrogen ions in a solution involving water. Each step increase in pH means a ten fold decrease in the concentration of hydrogen ions in the solution. Thus a solution of pH 6 has 10 times the concentration of hydrogen ions than one at pH 7 and 1000 times the hydrogen ion concentration as one at pH 8.0

Pheromone. A chemical produced by an organism that influence the behavior or physiology of another member of the same species. Thus the chemicals ants use for their ant trails would be pheromones. People tend to think of pheromones as sex attractants but most pheromones work in other contexts. Also humans do have sex pheromones but because of our relative intelligence, attraction involves a few more characteristics than the right smell.

Phloem. The set of complex plant tissues involved in the transport of sugars and other organic compounds throughout the plant. Contrast **xylem.**

Phospholipid. A compound consisting of two fatty acid chains linked to a glycerol molecule. The top position in the glycerol molecule is occupied by a polar group consisting in part of a phosphate functional group along with any one of a number of other functional groups. The result is a molecule with two hydrophobic tails (the fatty acids) and a polar head(the phosphate containing group).

Phosphoprotein. A conjugated protein formed by the combination of protein with phosphate groups.

Photic zone. The surface layer of an ocean or lake that is penetrated by sunlight and in which the phytoplankton flourish. Red and yellow wavelength of light penetrate to about 50 m while blue and violet light may reach 200 m. The diatoms, which are the main components of phytoplankton, may be found down to 80 m. Beyond 200 m the water is perpetually dark.

Photon. A discrete packet or quantum of light energy. Remember light can viewed as a wave or a particle. When we talk about light as being absorbed by electrons many time we treat light as a photon.

Photonasty. A nastic movement in response to change in light intensity.

Photolysis. The process by which water is split during the light dependent reactions of photosynthesis. The purpose of this process is to replenish electrons lost by the photosystems. In addition the process produces hydrogen ions which are used to help make ATP by electron transport phosphorylation and oxygen which has been exploited by many organisms for cellular respiration.

Photophosphorylation. The conversion of ADP to ATP using light energy.

Photoreceptor. Any light-sensitive organ or organelle. The eyes of vertebrates and the ocelli and compound eyes of insects are photoreceptors, as are the organelles of such protoctists as Euglena.

Photosystem. A series of pigments called antenna pigments and with a chlorophyll molecule that absorb light which boosts electrons to a high energy level where they can be picked up by NADP+ as part of the light dependent reactions of photosynthesis.

Phototaxis. A taxis in response to light. Many motile algae are positively phototactic, e.g. Volvox, while cockroaches are examples of negatively phototactic organisms.

Phototropism. The bending of a plant toward or away from light. The shoot is typically positively phototropic while the roots are often negatively **phototropic**.

Phosphate. An important functional group consisting of a phosphorus atom and three oxygen's.

Phragmoplast. A barrel-shaped body apearing in dividing plant cells during late anaphase and telophase between the two separating groups of chromosomes. It consists of microtubules associated with the spindle, and transports vesicle that coalesce to form the early cell plate.

Phyletic. Relating to or reflecting the evolutionary history of an organism. Some developmental structures or processes, such as gill pouches in mammal embryos, are regarded as phyletic, Phyletic classifications are based on the assumed evolutionary relationships between organisms rather than their observable characteristics.

Phylloclade. A type of cladode in which the flattened or globose stem has taken over the photosynthetic function of the leaves, which are reduced to spines or scales. It is often an adaption to prevent water loss and is seen in certain xerophytic plants, e.g. prickly pear.

Phyllode. An expanded flattened petiole that acts as the photosynthetic organ if the latmina is missing or very reduced. Phyllodes are seen in the Australian acacia.

Phylogeny. The evolutionary history of a species or other group of organisms.

Phylum. One of the major groups into which a kingdom of organism is classified. Phyla may be divided into subphyla. In some plant classifications the term 'division' is used instead of phylum.

Physiology. The way in which organisms or parts of organisms function.

Phytoalexin. A nonspecific antibiotic produced by a plant, usually in response to infection by a fungus or to injury.

Pia mater. The innermost of the three membranes that surround the brain and spinal cord of vertebrates. The pia mater lies immediately adjacent to the central nervous system, and the choroid plexus, which secretes cerebrospinal fluid, is an extension of it.

Picornavirus. One of a group of small RNA-containing viruses commonly present in the alimentary and respiratory tracts of vertebrates. They cause mild infections of these tracts but the group also includes the polioviruses, which attack the central nervous system causing poliomyelitis; and the aphthoviruses responsible for foot and mouth disease in cattle, sheep, and pigs.

Pie chart. A diagram in which percentages are shown as sectors of a circle. If x present of the prey of a carnivore comprises species X, y percent species Y, and z percent species Z, a pie chart would show three sectors having central angles 3.6 x Degree, 3.6 y Degree, and 3.6 z Degree.

Pigment. A compound that appears white, black or colored due to the patterns of absorption and reflection of light hitting the molecules of the compound. Examples include various dyes, chlorophyll, and melanin

Pileus. The umbrella-shaped cap of certain fungi, such as mushrooms. Spores are produced from gills or pores on the lower surface.

Piliferous layer. The part of the root epidermis that bears root hairs. It extends over a region about 4-10 mm behind the root tip. Beyond this the piliferous layer is sloughed off to reveal the hypodermis.

Pilomotor. Describing nerve fibres or the muscles invertebrated by them that can cause the position of the body hair to be altered. The arrector pili is a pilomotor muscle.

Pineal gland. An endocrine gland in the vertebrate forebrain that secretes melatonin and is involved with regulation of daily rhythms.

Pinna. The visible part of the outer ear, present in some mammals. It is made of cartilage and its function is to channel sound waves into the external auditory meatus. In some species the pinna is movable and aids in detecting the direction from which a sound originates.

Pinocytosis. The active taking in of bulk fluids by a cell using endocytosis. The term literally means "cell drinking."

Pipette. A graduated tube used for transferring measured volumes of liquid.

Pistil. The female reproductive parts of the flower and consisting of one or more carpels.

Pitfall trap. A simple trap for small invertebrate animals consisting of a tin that is placed in the ground with its rim at ground level. The trap, which contains some kind of bait, can be covered by a tile suspended above ground level hy stones so that rain does not enter the tin.

Pituitary gland. An important endocrine gland associated with and largely controlled by, the hypothalamus that secretes a wide range of hormones largely for the control of other endocrine glands.

Placentation. (Bot.) Manner in which the ovules are attached in an ovary.

Placodermi. Class of fossil bony fish, some large predators, mainly from the Devonian period. Bony shields on head and front part of body. AUTOSTYLIC JAW SUSPENSION; paired fins; heterocercal tail. Possibly related more to Chondrichtypes than to Osteichthyes or Acanthodil.

Plagioclimax. Any plant community whose composition is more or less stable and in equilibrium under existing conditions but which, as a result of human intervention, has not achieved the natural CLIMAX; e.g. grassland under continuous pasture.

Plagiosere. Succession of plants deflected into a new course through human intervention.

Planarians. Free-living members of the PLATYHELMINTHES. Class Turbellaria.

Plantation. Dichotomies in two or more planes, flattening out into one plane, e.g. a leaf.

Plantae. One of the five recognized kingdoms. Most plants except for a few parasitic plants are photosynthetic autotrophs and carry out photosynthesis using specialized organelles called chloroplasts. All plants have Eukaryotic cells and have cell walls made of a polysaccharide called cellulose. Plant life cycles involve alternation of generations. This type of life cycle gets its name because it alternates between spore producing sporophytes and gamete producing gametophytes.

Plant geography. Study of plant distributions, past and present, and of their causes.

Includes such fields as geology, palaeonthology, plant genetics, evolution and taxonomy.

Plantigrade. Mode of walking involving the central surface of the whole foot, i.e. the metacarpus or metatarsus and digits. Humans are plantigrade.

Plant sociology. Study of plant COMMUNITIES comprising the vegetation, their origins, compositions and structures.

Planula. Solid free-swimming ciliated larva of most classes of Cnidaria and a few of the Ctenophora. Composed of an outer ectoderm and inner endoderm, the latter formed by migration of cells into the interior.

Plasma. The fluid portion of blood.

Plasma cell. One kind of mature B CELL, active in antibody secretion.

Plasmagel. The gel-like state of the outer cytoplasm of many cells, as distinct from the more fluid inner cytoplasm with which it is intercon-vertible. May be highly vacuolated in planktonic protozoans. Involved in several forms of CELL LOCOMOTION, notably amoeboid locomotion.

Plasmodesmata. Channels through the cell walls of a plant cell that allow movement of chemicals between adjacent plant cells. Thus the cytoplasm of a whole series of plant cells may be continuously interconnected by the plasmodesmata. Such an interconnected group of cells called a **symplast** is critical for sugar transport.

Plasma membrane. A phospholipid bilayer and associated proteins that serves either as an outer cell membrane or one of the cell's internal membranes.

Plasmid. A small circular piece of DNA found in bacterial cells and that can be swapped with plasmids from other bacterial. Plasmids are important in genetic engineering because they can take up DNA from other organisms.

Plasmodium. 1. Genetic name of malarial parasites. 2. Vegetative stage of slimefungi. Multinucleate, amoeboid mass of protoplasm bounded by a plasma membrane but lacking definite shape or size.

Plasmogamy. Union of two or more protoplasts, typically of gametes, unaccompanied by union of any nuclei they may have.

Plasmolysis. The shrinking away of the cell membrane from the cell wall of plants by osmosis when the plant cell is placed in a hypertonic solution.

Plastid. Any of several DNA containing organelles found in plants and some protists that are involved in photosynthesis, starch storage and pigmentation.

Platyrrhines. Members of the anthropoid Infra-order Platyrrhini. Probably isolated from other primates since the Eocene. Characterized by broad nasal septum; 36teeth; often have prehensile tails. Include marmosets, tamarins, howler monkeys.

Plecoptera. Stoneflies. Small order of exopterygote insects with aquatic nymphs, long antennae, biting mouthparts and weak flight. Two pairs of wings, held flat over back at rest; hind pair usually larger. Adults tend to feed on lichens and unicellular algae. Good pollution indicators.

Plectenchyma. Tissue composed of fungal hyphae; either prosenchyma, in which component hyphae are loosely woven and recognizable as such, or pseudoparenchyma comprising closely-packed cells which can no longer be distinguished as hyphae and resemble parenchyma of higher-plants.

Pleiomorphism. Form of POLYMORPHISM in which there are several different forms in the LIFE CYCLE; e.g. in the life cycles of rust fungi, where there is a succession of different spore forms.

Pleiotropic. Refers to a gene having more than one affect on the phenotype of an organism.

Plesiomorphic. In PHYLOGENETICS, describing the original pre-existing member of a pair of homologous characters, the evolutionary noveity being the apomorphic member of the pair.

Plesiosauria. Extinct suborder of marine euryapsid reptiles, prominent in the Mesozoic. Typical length 3 metres; long-necked, short-bodied, with limbs modified into powerful paddles. Derived from similar nothosaurs, they were not dinosaurs.

Pleura. Serous membranes lining PLEURAL CAVITY and covering the lung surfaces in mammals. Normally only a thin fluid layer separates the pleura from body wall.

Pleural cavity. Coelomic space surrounding each lung in a mammal, separated from rest of periviseral coelom by the diaphragm. Pleural cavities are separated from each other by mediastinum and the pericardium.

Pleurocarpus. Growth form in some mosses, where the gametophore is multi-branched and creeping, with the sporophyte borne upon a very short lateral branch.

Pliocene. The last epoch of the TERTIARY period, during which the first HOMINOIDS appeared. Deserts formed. The climate became cooler, and widespread glaciation occurred in the Northern Hemisphere. Much uplift and mountain formation occurred; Panama joined North and South Americans.

Ploidy. The number of haploid chromosome sets in a nucleus, or cell. A haploid nucleus has a ploidy of 1. a diploid nucleus 2. a triploid nucleus 3. etc. The ploidy of a eukaryotic cell influences its volume, approximately proportionately.

Plurilocular. Possessing many chambers, e.g. describing gametangia and mitosporangia in brown algae.

Pluteus. Larva of echinoid or ophiuroid. Ciliated and planktonic.

Pneumatocyst. Hollow region of stipes of some brown algae, containing gas helping to keep the alga afloat.

Polar covalent bond. A bond involving atoms that have a relatively strong tendency to grab electrons and atoms with a tendency to give up electrons. The premier example is water. The oxygen molecule has a strong tendency to take electrons and hydrogen has a strong tendency to give it electron up. The result is a molecule that is slightly negative on one side and slightly positive on the other side.

Polar molecules. are molecules in which one end has a positive charge, another end has a negative charge. Polar molecules can also arise from the presence of ions.

Polar nuclei. Two haploid nuclei in the centre of the embryo sac of flowering plants. These nuclei fuse with a male gamete nucleus to form a triploid endosperm nucleus, which subsequetly divides to form the endosperm.

Pollen sac. The structure in seed plants in which pollen is produced. In angiosperms there are usually four pollen sacs in each anther; they contain the mirospore mother cells. In gymnosperms variable numbers of pollen sacs are borne on the microsporophylls that make up the male cone.

Pollex. The innermost digit on the forelimb of a tetrapod vertebrate. It contains two phalanges and in humans and higher primates it is the thumb, which is opposable and gives the hand greater manipulating ability. In some mammals a pollex is absent.

Pollutant. Any substance, produced and released into the environment as a result of human activities, that has damaging effects on living organisms. Pollutants may be toxic substances or natural constituents of the atmosphere that are present inexcessive amounts.

Polycistronic. Describing a type of messenger RNA that can encode more than one polypeptide separately within the same RNA molecule. Bacteria messenger RNA is generally polycistronic.

Polyembryony. 1. The formation of more than one embryo in a plant seed. Often one embryo develops from the fertilized egg cell, while the others have formed asexually from other tissue in the ovule. 2. The formation of more than one embryo from a single animal zygote. Identical twins are produced in this way.

Polygene. Any of a group of genes influencing a quantitative trait, such as height in humans.

Polygenic inheritance. refers to a situation where a trait such as height or weight is controlled not by genes at a single locus, but by inputs from many loci. Many seemingly continuous phenotypic characteristics are controlled at least in part in this way.

Polymer. A polymer is a large molecule made out of repeating molecular subunits. These subunits may be exactly the same as in cellulose which is made out of thousands of repeating glucose subunits, or they may be similar as in the case of proteins which are made out of slightly different amino acid subunits strung together like slightly different box cars of a train.

Polymerases. A series of enzymes responsible for taking nucleotides and producing nucleic acids. DNA polymerase catalyses the formation of DNA during DNA replication. RNA polymerase is responsible for catalyzing the production of the RNA transcript during transcription.

Polypeptide. A series of many amino acids linked together by peptide bonds. Larger polypeptides are called proteins but to a large degree the terms are used interchangeably.

Polyploidy. A situation where the cells of an organism have more than two of each kind of homologous chromosome. This is common in plants. The triploid (three copies of each chromosome) and tetraploid (four copies) are the most common forms of polyploidy

Polysepalous. Describing a flower that possesses a calyx consisting of separate sepals.

Polyspermy. The entry of several sperms into the egg during fertilization although only one sperm nucleus actually fuses with the egg nucleus. Polyspermy occurs in animals with yolky eggs.

Polythetic. Describing a type of classification in which membership of a taxon is based on its constituent organisms sharing a large number of characteristics.

Polytopic. Describing a taxon that has arisen and exists in more than one geographical region.

Polytypic. Describing a species that exists in a variety of forms or subspecies that inhabit different geographical regions.

Pome. A type of fruit characteristic of apples and pears. The flesh of the fruit develops from the receptacle of the flower, which completely encloses the fused carpels. After fertilization the carpels form the core of the fruit, which contains the seeds.

Pons. A thick tract of nerve fibres in the brain that links the medulla oblongata to the midbrain. Its function is to relay impulses between different parts of the brain. The pons is named after its discoverer, the Italian anatomist C. Varoli (1543-75).

Population. A population is a group of organisms of the same species living in a well defined area.

Portal system. Refers to two sets of capillaries connected by a vein as in hepatic portal system.

Precipitin. An antibody that combines with and precipitates soluble antigen, used in the precipitin reaction for identifying antigens.

Premaxilla. A paired membrane bone forming the anterior region of the upper jaw in most vertebrates. In mammals, it bears the incisor teeth.

Premolar. A mammalian tooth situated between the canine teeth or incisors in front and the molars behind. Premolars are multiple-rooted and ridged and are used for grinding food.

Presumptive. Describing embryonic tissues that are presumed to develop in certain way. For example, presumptive neural plate of amphibians lies towards the animal pole of the blastula.

Prickle. A protective outgrowth from the surface of a plant. It may be a modified trichome and thus completely epidermal in origin, or it may also contain cortical and vascular tissue.

Primary growth. Growth derived solely from meristems present in the embryo, i.e. apical meristems. Such growth generally increases the length of plant organs.

Primary plant body. The structure that is derived solely from meristems present in the embryo and their derivatives.

Primary structure. A description of a protein solely in terms of the sequence of amino acids and the position of certain chemical bonds, usually disulfide bonds. Insulin is shown here. Note that it consists of two polypeptide chains:

Chain 1 GLY -ILE -VAL-GLU -GLN -CYS -CYS -THR-SER -ILE -CYS- SER -LEU -TYR -GLN -LEU -GLU -ASN -TYR -CYS -ASN

Chain 2 PHE -VAL -ASN-GLN -HIS -LEU -CYS- GLY-ASP -HIS -LEU- VAL- GLU-ALA -LEU- TYR -LEU- VAL-CYS- GLY- GLU- ARG -GLY-PHE -PHE -TYR - THR -PRO -LYS -THR

Data from the Brookhaven Protein Data Base.

Primary tissue. Plant tissue that is derived solely from meristems present in the embryo and their derivatives.

Principle of Superposition. The idea that in deposits of sedimentary rock the oldest deposits are on the bottom and the youngest deposits are on the top. This an important concept in dating the relative age of fossils and in reconstructing geological history.

Prokaryotic cell. Refers to a cell that lacks a nucleus and other membrane bound membranes. Bacteria and archea are prokaryotes. Contrast with **eukaryotic cell**.

Protein. A protein is a compound made from smaller molecules called amino acids. The amino acids are strung together by specialized chemical bonds called peptide bonds. Proteins serve many important functions in the organism.

Protista. One of the currently recognized kingdoms of living things. The protista are single celled or primitively multicellular organisms, characterized by having membrane bound organelles and a true nucleus. Paramecium, Euglena, Amoeba, Stentor, Algae and Diatoms are representative Protists. The Protists are considered to be a catch all group for organisms that don't fit into the other kingdoms.

Proton. A positively charged particle found in the nucleus of an atom. The number of protons in the nucleus of the atom is equal to the number of electrons surrounding the nucleus.

Pseudoallele. A mutation in a gene that produces an effect identical to another mutation at a different site in the same gene locus. The two pseudoalleles thus act as a single gene but do not occupy the same position, as evidenced by the occasional rare recombinations between them that result in the cistrans effect.

Pseudocarp. A fruit that includes other parts of the flower, e.g. the bracts, inflorescence, or receptacle, in addition to the ovary.

Pseudopodium. A temporary finger-like projection or lobe on the body of an ameboid cell. It is formed by a flowing action of the cytoplasm and functions in locomotion and feeding.

Psychrophilic. Describing microorganisms that can live at temperatures below 20 Degree C.

Ptyalin. An enzyme present in the saliva of humans and some animals. It belongs to the group of carbohydrate-hydrolyzing enzymes known as amylases. It catalyzes the conversion of starch to maltose.

Ptyxis. The way in which young leaves are folded or rolled in the bud.

Public symphysis. A joint formed by the union of the two public bones at the midventral line of the pelvic girdle of mammals and many reptiles. It is slightly deformed in mammals during labor, in order to case passage of the fetus.

Pubis. One of a pair of bones forming the anterior ventral portion of the tetrapod pelvic girdle. They are sometimes joined at the public symphysis.

Punctuated equilibrium. Refers to the idea that the evolutionary history of species has long periods where no evolution happens interspersed with brief bursts of evolutionary change.

Pure covalent bond. A chemical bond between two or more atoms that involves a more or less equal sharing of electrons among the atoms. Carbon is capable of forming large covalently bonded structures.

Pylorus. A ring of involuntary muscle in vertebrates that surrounds the opening from the stomach to the duodenum. It regulates the passage of food between stomach and duodenum.

Pyruvic acid (pyruvate). A three carbon organic acid that is a product of glycolysis.

Pyrimidine. A simple nitrogenous organic molecule whose ring structure is contained in the pyrimidine bases cytosine, thymine, and uracil, which are constituents of the nucleic acids, and in thiamine.

Q

Quadrat. An ecological sampling unit consisting of a small square area of ground within which all species of interest are noted of measurements taken. Quadrats may be spaced over a larger area to form an overall view when a total survey would be used to sample along a transect.

Quadrate. A paired bone in the upper jaw of bony fishes, amphibians, reptiles, and birds that articulates with the lower jawbone. It is absent in mammals, being reduced to a small bone in the middle ear.

Quadriceps. A group of extensor muscles that cover the anterior surface and sides of the mammalian femur, These muscles joint at the base and are connected to the tibia by a single tendon. Muscle spindles in the quadriceps are responsible for the kneejerk reflex.

Quantitative inheritance. The determination of a particular characteristic, e.g. height or skin colour, by many genes, each having a small effect individually. Characteristics controlled in this way show continuous variation.

Quantitative structure-activity relationship (QSAR). A statistical algorithm that quantitatively defines the relationship between the chemical structure of a drug and its effect on an organism. QSRA studies are often used to predict the activity or toxicity of new drugs. Similar methods can be used to predict the metabolism of new drugs.

Quantitative trait. Any phenotypic trait that shows continuous variation and can be measured quantitatively in terms of length, weight, concentration, test score, etc. Such traits, which include height, intelligence, and obesity, are determined by the cumulative effects of numerous genes at quantitative trait loci.

Quantitative trait locus (QTL). A region of a chromosome containing one or more genes that contribute to determining a quantitative trait. Typically, several or many such genes, each having a small effect, act together to specify the trait.

Quarantine. A period of isolation imposed on an animal that moves from an area where particular diseases are prevalent to an area where those diseases are not prevalent. In the UK domestic animals or livestock entering the occury are quarantined for the necessary incubation period in order to prevent the spread of a particular disease.

Quaternary structure. The fourth level of protein structure. This arises when different protein molecules come together to form a larger unit. For example, Hemoglobin actually is composed of four protein units. The ultimate in quaternary structure may be the microtubules in the cytoskeleton which are made of 10's of thousands of protein units, each unit being a molecule of a protein called tubulin. Actually each tubulin itself is composed of two protein sub units. So what do we call this "Quintary structure??"

Quiescent centre. Area at the tip of the root apical meristem where rate of cell division is lower than in surrounding tissue.

Quinine. An important alkaloid extracted from the bark of Cinchona species used in the treatment of malaria.

Quinoa. Chenopodium quinoa is an important grain crop in the Andes, and elsewhere in South America.

Quinone. Any of various compounds derived from benzene and containing C=O groups in an unsaturated ring. An example is plastoquinone.

R

Rachis. 1. Main axis of an INFLORESCENCE. 2. The axis of a fern leaf (frond), from which the pinnae arise. 3. In compound leaves, the extension of the petiole corresponding to the midrib of an entire leaf.

Radial section. Longitudinal section cut parallel to the radius of a chylindrical body (e.g. stem or root).

Radial symmetry. A body plan in which the body parts originate from the central of the organism like spokes in a wheel. Star fish and jellyfish and among the creatures which share this type of symmetry.

Radical. Root of embryo seed plants.

Radius. One of two long bones in the tetrapod forelimb. Articulates with the side of the fore-foot bearing the thumb.

Radula. 'Tongue' of molluscs; a horny strip, continually renewed, with teeth on its surface for rasping food. Found in Amphineura, Gastropoda and Cephalopoda; absent in Bivalvia, which are microphagous. May be modified for borning in some species. Patteren of teeth helpful in identification.

RAGE (receptor for advanced glycation end-products). A cells surface receptor protein of the immunoglobulin superfamily which binds potentially damaged glycated proteins.

Ramet. An offshort or module in some plants and modular invertebrates, formed by vegetative growth, and actually or potentially capable of independent physiological existence (e.g. tubers of a potato plants, the polyps on a colonial hydroid).

Raphe. 1. In seeds formed from anatropous ovules, a longitudinal ridge marking position of the adherent FUNICLE. 2. Elongated slit through valve wall of some pennate diatoms, involved in movement of cell over the substratum.

Rarity. A growing body of evidence suggests that locally rate species tend to share some or all of the following characteristics compared with commoner taxa: (i) lower levels of self-incompatibility, (ii) tendency towards asexual reproduction, (iii) lower overall reproductive effort, and (iv) poorer dispersal abilities.

Ras genes. Oncogenes initially discovered through their ability to cause RAT sarcomas. Mutations in ras in mammalian cells tend to be oncogenic acid are frequently associated with human cancers. Encode RAS PROTEINS.

Ray. (Bot.) Tissue initiated by CAMBIUM and extending radially in secondary xylem and phloem. Mainly parenchymatous, but may include tracheids in the xylem. (Zool).

Ray initials. (Bot.) One of two types of meristematic cells of the vascular cambium; horizontally elongated or squarish cells that produce horizontally orientated ray cells, which form the vascular rays, or radial system. The rays, composed largely of parenchyma cells, are variable in length.

RdRP. RNA-directed RNA polymerase. Converts single-stranded RNA into double stranded RNA . Some viruses encode their own. Apparently not encoded by the human genome. RdRP also has a surveillance role in Neurospora by silencing unpaired DNA during meiosis-unpaired genes probably being foreign DNA sequences, such as transports

Reaction centre. (Bot.) The chlorophyll molecule of photo-system capable of using energy in the photochemical reaction.

Receptor serine/threonine kinases. Transmembrane receptors found, with distinctions, in both the plant and animal kingdoms. All have an intracellular serine/threonine kinase domain and an extracellular ligand-binding domain. Unlike animals, plants seem to depend more on these receptors than they do on the RECEPTOR TYROSINE KINASES.

Recessive allele. An alternate form of a gene that has no obvious effect on the phenotype of a heterozygous individual.

Recombination. A name given for one of any number of processes in prokaryotes and eukaryotes that serve to produce new combinations of genetic material already existing in individuals. Thus crossing over and independent assortment would be examples of recombination in meiosis. Sexual reproduction as a whole is a type of recombination.

Rectum. Terminal part of intestine, opening via anus or cloaca and commonly storing faeces. In insects, often reabsorbs water, salts amd amino acids from the 'urine'; some insect larvae have tracheal gills in the rectum, while larva; dragonflies also eject water forcibly from the rectum for propulsion. Ectodermal in origin.

Redia. One of the larval types in endoparasitic Trematoda, developing asexually from the sporocyst and from other rediae. Often parasitic in snails, developing into cercariae.

Reducing sugar. A sugar capable of reducing ferric or cupric ion in solution, as indicated by BENEDICT'S TEST. Depends upon presence of potentially free aldehyde or ketone group. Most monosaccharides are reducing sugars, as are most disaccharides except sucrose.

Reduction. The addition of electrons and often hydrogen ions to a substance. Contrast oxidation.

Reduction division. First division of MEIOSIS, the chromosome numbers of the daughter cells produced being half that of the parent cell.

Reflex. An automatic response to a stimulus consisting usually of a small number of steps, perhaps just a muscle twitch. A motor program as an elaborate sequence of automatic responses is become a common term. However, the distinction is not always clear cut.

Refugium. Locality which has escaped drastic alteration following climatic change, in contrast to the region as a whole. Refugia usually form centres for RELIC species populations or communities.

Regulatory proteins. Proteins which activate, suppress or otherwise modulate gene expression and metabolic pathways. Usually allosteric, they may in turn be modulated by phosphorylation or covalent modification. Important functional classes include REGULATORY ENZYMES, caspases and TRANSCRIPTION FACTORS.

Releaser. A general term for a stimulus that triggers a fixed action pattern.

Releasing factor. Substance stimulating release of hormone into blood. The locus classicus for their production is the vertebrate HYPOTHALAMUS, several of whose neurosecretions initiate hormone release from the anterior pitutary.

Relic. 1. Surviving organism, population or community characteristic of an earlier time. 2. A relic distribution of fauna of flora is one representing the localized remains of an originally much widerranging distribution such as those organisms, now confined to mountain tops, which were far more widespread in glacial times.

Renin. Enzyme produced by juxtaglomerular cells of kidney when blood pressure falls.

Replicon. Nucleic acid molecule containing a nucleotide sequence forming a replication origin, at which replication is initiated. Usually one per bacterial or viral genome, but often several per eukaryotic chromosome.

Reproduction. The production of new individuals physically independent of their parents.

Reproductive allocation. The proportion of an organism's available resource input that is allocated to reproduction over a defined period of time. Often this is the proportion of an organism's biomass or volume that is reproductive tissue.

Reproductive cost. The decrease in survivorship and/or growth rate, and therefore the decrease in the potential for future reproduction, suffered by an individual as a result of increasing its current allocation to reproduction.

Reproductive success. Just as it sounds this term refers to the number of offspring an organism has. This is not the same as fitness which is reproductive success relative to the other members of the population.

Resin duct. Relatively large intercellular spaces lined by thin-walled parenchyma cells secreting resin into the duct. Wounding pressure, frost and wind damage can stimulate their formation. Resin apparently protects the plant from attack by decay fungi and bark beetles. Found i n conifers.

Resource. Whatever is consumed by one organism and, as a result, becomes unavailable to another. When limiting, results in COMPETITION. Light may be a requirement but, although sometimes limiting, is not strictly a resource.

Resource depletion zone. The region around a consumer in which the availability of a RESOURCE is reduced (e.g. the zone surrounding the absorbing surface of a root from which nutrients and water are absorbed).

Respiration. This term has two uses: **Cellular respiration** refers to the oxidation of food stuffs to produce ATP. **Respiration** also refers to gas exchange (releasing Carbon dioxide and taking in oxygen)between the organism and the environment.

Restriction enzymes. A class of enzymes found in bacteria that cut strands of DNA at sites determined by certain base sequences. In nature, these enzymes help the bacteria cope with and manipulate foreign DNA. These enzymes are important tools in genetic engineering because they help scientists isolate DNA fragments containing genes.

Retrovirus. An RNA virus that uses an enzyme called reverse transcriptase to make a DNA molecule, sometimes called copy DNA, which then gets inserted into the host cell's genetic material.

Reverse transcriptase. An enzyme found in retroviruses that enables the production of a DNA copy from the viral RNA. Since the usual flow of information in living things is from DNA to an RNA transcript these enzymes are called "reverse" transcriptase.

Rhizoid. A unicellular root-like structure found in certain algae and in the gametophyte generation of the bryophytes and some pteridophytes. It serves to anchor the plant and absorb water and nutrients.

Rhizome. A stem that grows horizontally below ground. Rhizomes may be Fleshy or wiry (e.g. couch grass) and may serve as an organ of perennation or vegetative propagation, or occasionally both.

Rhizomorph. A structure found in certain fungi (e.g. Agaricus) consisting of a mass of hyphae forming a complex strand of tissue that serves to transport food from one part of the mycelium to another, thus aiding propagation.

Rhizophore. An organ found only in Selaginella species that arises just beyond each fork of the stem. It resembles a root in being positively geotrophic and having a similar internal anatomy. However it arises exogenously and lacks a root cap. True roots develop endogenously from the tip of the rhizoophore.

Ribonucleic acid. A single stranded nucleic acid containing ribose and using uracil in place of thymine. Various RNA's are involved in protein synthesis and comprise the genetic material of certain viruses including the **retroviruses**.

Ribose. A five carbon monosaccaride best known for its role as a component of nucleotides and the nucleic acid RNA. A related monosaccharide, differing by lacking an oxygen, is called deoxyribose. This sugar is found in DNA.

Ribosome. A very small two part organelle containing RNA and proteins that is involved in the translation step of protein synthesis. In eukaryotic cells, ribosomes may be free in the cytoplasm or bound to the surface of the **rough endoplasmic reticulum(Rough ER)**.

Ribosomal RNA. The RNA found as part of the ribosome and that serve in part as a ribozyme involved in forming peptide bonds.

Ribozyme. An RNA molecule that serves as an enzyme. The Ribosomal RNA in the ribosome acts as an enzyme to catalyze the formation of peptide bonds during protein synthesis

Rickets. A childhood condition caused by decalicification of bone, resulting in deformed bones. Rickets is associated with chronic deficiency of vitamin D or calcium and with disorders that cause poor phosphate reabsorption from the kidney nephrons.

Rigor mortis. The stiffening of the body of an animal after death, due to a temporary rigidity of the muscles. This condition arises because ATP, which is no longer synthesized after death, is required to break down the bridges that form between actin and myosin filaments inmuscle tissue during contraction.

Ringer's solution. Physilogical saline; aqueous solution, containing sodium, potassium and calcium chlorides, employed in maintaning cells or organs alive in vitro. Always appropriately buffere, usually with bicarbonate or phosphate.

Ring-porous wood. Secondary XYLEM in which the vessels of the early wood, when viewed in cross-section, are distinctly larger than those of the late wood and form a well-defined zoon or ring.

Ring species. Species characterized by circular of looped geographical distributions, adjacent populations interbreeding on the two arms of the loop but not where arms overlap, i.e. those populations presumably furthest from the original area of spread.

Ritualized behaviour. Behaviour which has become stereotyped in evolution through its role in communication. Many display and threat sequences are ritualized and some DISPLACEMENT ACTIVITIES have become so through selection as information-bearers.

Ritualization. An evolutionary process in which the form or context of an action is altered because it comes to play a role in social communication. For example, many courtship and greeting ceremonies in animals include ritual food presentation, derived from the action of feeding the young.

RNA-binding proteins. Proteins with at least one RNA-binding motif (RBM), encoded by members of the RMB gene family. Involved in RNA transport and processing.

RNA interference (RNAi). A form of RNA SILENCING occurring in the cells of most, if not all, multicellular eukaryotes and an effective method of GENE SILENCING. It ensures that a specific mRNA molecule is destroyed and has great potential as a tool in biological research and can be tailored for the suppression of any gene, possibly even viral ones.

RNase. Any of several enzymes which hydrolyse RNA by breaking their phosphodiester bonds.

RNA splicing. The joining together of RNA sequences on either side of intron sequences after the latter have been removed during RNA PROCESSING. Alternative RNA splicing is responsible for the production of the various immunoglobulin like NCAMs, the splicing steps taking place in the SPLICEOSOME, catalysed by small nuclear RNAs (snRNAs).

Rod. A type of light-sensitive receptor cell present in the retinas of vertebrates. Rods contain the pigment rhodopsin and are essential for vision in dim light. They are not evenly distributed on the retina, being absent in the fovea and occupying all of the retina margin.

Roentgen. The former unit of dose equivalent. It is named after the discoverer of X-rays, W.K.Roentgen.

Root cap. A cone-shaped structure that covers the root tip and develops as a result of cell division by a meristem at the root apex. It protects the root tip as it grows between the soil particles. The cells are constantly worn away be friction and are replaced by the meristem.

Root mass ratio. The dry mass of the roots of a plant divided by the total dry mass of the entire plant. typically measured in grams per gram or kilograms per kilogram. This reflects the production of resources that a plant allocates to its root system, which varies with such factors as species, growing conditions, and season.

Root nodule. A swelling on the roots of certain plants, especially those of the family Fabaceae, that contains bacteria capable of fixing atmospheric nitrogen into ammonia, which is subsequently converted to nitrates and amino acids. Plants that possess root nodules increase soil fertility by increasing the nitrate content of the soil. The practice of crop rotation will normally include the cultivation of a leguminous species. Certain nonleguminous plants, such as alder and bayberry, also form root nodules, although the bacteria are filamentous actinomycetes not rhizobia.

Root pressure. The pressure that forces water, absorbed from the soil, to move through the roots and up the stem of a plant. This pressure can be demonstrated by cutting a stem, from which water will exude. A manometer can be attached to a plant stem to measure the root pressure. Root pressure is believed to be due to both the osmosis of water, from the soil into the root cells, and the active pumping of salts into the xylem tissue, which maintains a concentration gradient along which the water will move.

Rotifera. A phylum of microscopic pseudocoelomate aquatic animals characterized by a crown of cilia at the head end. these are used in locomotion and in some species for feeding; the crown resembles a rotating wheel when the cilia are beating. Rotifers possess jaws and are covered with a layer of chitin. There is no circulatory system and gas exchange occurs across the body surface. Some rotifers reproduce by parthenogenesis.

Round window. A membrane-covered opening between the middle ear and the inner ear, situated below the oval window. Pressure waves transmitted through the perilymph in the cochlea are released into the middle ear through the round window, which bulges out into the middleear cavity.

Royal jelly. A highly nutritious food substance that is secreted from the hypo-pharyngeal and mandibular glands of worker honeybees and fed to the newly hatched larvae. For the first three days after hatching larvae that will develop into worker bees are fod on royal jelly, after which their diet changes to pollen and nectar. However, larvae that will develop into queen bees continue to be fed exclusively on royal jelly throughout the larval stage.

RuBP. Ribulose bi phosphate. A five carbon sugar with two phosphate groups that is the starting material for the Calvin cycle. Carbon dioxide is attached to this compound to form a six carbon unstable intermediate which breaks into two three carbon molecules of PGA.

Ruderal. Describing a plant species that is characteristic of land with a high level of disturbance (e.g. resulting from environmental disaster or human activity) but rich in resources (water, nutrients, etc.). Such species tend to quickly colonize bare patches and reproduce rapidly, but are poor completitors against more robust species.

Rumen. The second of four chambers that form the stomach of ruminants.

Runner. A stem that grows horizontally along the soil surface and gives rise to new plants either from axilary or terminal buds. Runners are seen in the creeping buttercup and the strawberry. Offsets, e.g. those of the houseleek, are short runners.

Rusts. A group of parasitic fungi of the phylum Basidiomycota. Many of these species attack the leaves and stems of cereal crops; characteristic rust-coloured streaks of spores appear on infected plants. The life cycles of some rusts may be complex; many form a number of different types of spore and some require two different host plants.

Rough endoplasmic reticulum (Rough ER). A network of membranous sacs connected to the nuclear envelope that is covered with ribosomes. Rough ER is a site for active synthesis and collection of proteins.

S

Saccharide. A saccharide is a simple sugar or compounds built from simple sugars. Saccharides consisting of one simple sugar unit are called monosaccharides. Those built from two sugar units are disaccharides. Those from more than two but not a whole bunch are oligosaccharides, and those saccharides built from many sugar units are called polysaccharides. Glucose and fructose are common monosaccharides. Linking these two together yield the common disaccharide, sucrose. Starch. Pectin and cellulose are common polysaccharides produced by plants. Glycogen is a polysaccharide produced by animals. All of these polysaccharides are polymers of glucose.

Saccharomyces. A genus of unicellular ascomycete fungi that can live in both aerobic and anaerobic conditions. They are important in the brewing and baking industries, respectively, for the alcohol and carbon dioxide they produce by anaerobic respiration. Reproduction is generally asexual by budding although in adverse conditions sexual spores may be formed. These years are also used in gene cloning as convenient eukaryotic hosts to express inserted foreign genes.

Sacculus. The lower chamber of the labyrinth of the vertebrate inner ear, which bears the hearing organ-the cochlea of reptiles, birds, and mammals. There is a patch of sensory epithelium in the wall lining and granules of calcium carbonate in the cavity, which together are responsible for the detection of changes in position of the head with respect to gravity and the rate of change.

Sacral vertebrae. Large strong vertebrae between the lumbar and coccygeal regions of the vertebral column that articulate with the pelvic girdle of tetrapods. There is one in amphibians and two or more in reptiles, birds, and mammals.

Sacrum. One or more fused sacral vertebrae in the lower back region that are attached to the ilia and give support to the pelvic girdle of tetrapods. In humans, the sacrum is a large tringular bony mass comprising five fused sacral vertebrae.

Saliva. A secretion produced by the salivary glands of animals, consisting mainly of mucus. It is used to moisten and lubricate the food and in some animals contains enzymes. For example, in humans and certain insects, the enzyme amylase is present and starts off the process of starch digestion. In some insects (e.g. mosquito) the saliva contains an anticoagulant.

Salivary glands. Glands that secrete a watery secretion into the buccal cavity. In the rabbit there are four pairs: parotid, infraorbital, submaxillary, and sublingual; in humans there are three pairs: parotid, submadibular, and sublingual.

Samara. A dry one-seeded indehiscent fruit with the pericarp extended into a membranous wing, e.g. the ash fruit.

Sand. Mineral particles consisting mainly of quartz, felspar, and mica, and measuring between 1.00 and 0.05 mm in diameter. Sandy soils are light and drain well. However, retention of nutrients is poor and such soils are often structureless and lose water quickly.

Saprophyte(saprobe). A fungus or bacteria that feeds on the remains of other organisms. Decomposer.

Saprozoic. Describing an organism that feeds on organic material in solution, rather than on solid organic material.

Sapwood. The outer living xylem cells in a tree trunk, consisting of xylem elements, parenchyma, and medullary rays, that are actively involved in water transport and food storage.

Sarcoplasm. The cytoplasm of the fibres of striated muscle, excluding the myofibrils.

Sarcoplasmic reticulum. A modified form of smooth endoplasmic reticulum found in striated and cardiac muscle, Muscle contraction requires calcium ions and the network of sarcoplasmic reticulum releases them quickly to all parts of the muscle fiber in response to nervous impulses. Calcium activates the enzyme AtPase, which catalyzes breakdown of ATP, thus releasing the energy required for contraction., After contraction, the sarcoplasmic reticulum reabsorbs the calcium.

Satellite DNA. A type of DNA that can be separated by centrifugation from the main DNA fraction. It includes DNA from the chromosomal region adjacent to the centromere, which has a base composition unlike that of most DNA, and DNA from mitochondria, chloroplasts, and ribosomes.

Saturated and Unsaturated. These terms refer to the number of available bonds for more hydrogens in a hydrocarbon or other organic compound. If the compound is saturated then all the available bonds are taken up by hydrogens and other atoms and there are only single bonds between the carbons. In unsaturated compounds, there are double bonds between at least two of the carbons which could be broken to add more hydrogens. Fats are typically saturated while oils are unsaturated.

Scalariform thickening. A type of secondary wall formation consisting of interlaced spiral bands of thickening giving a ladder-like formation. It is found in metaxylem tracheids and vessels.

Schizocarp. A dry fruit, formed from two or more carpels, the divides at maturity into one seeded achene-like segments termed mericarps. Such fruits are seen n hollyhock.

Schizogeny. The separation of plant cells at the middle lamellae to give intercellular spaces, which may have special functions.

Schultze's solution. A solution of zinc chloride, potassium iodine, and iodine used mainly for testing for cellulose and hemicellulose. Both materials stain a blue color with the reagent, that of hemicellulose being weaker.

Schwann cell. A cell that makes a section of the myelin sheath of a medullated nerve fiber. During development, the cell becomes spirally wrapped around the nerve fibre.

Science. Science is the systematic study of the natural world. Science involves the use of a systematic method called the **Scientific method** which has the following basic steps: Observation; question; hypothesis; prediction based on hypothesis; test(may involve experiment or more observations); conclusion(a judgment of the likelihood that the hypothesis is correct); communication to the outside world sufficient to allow others to repeat the test or build on the scientist's results This latter aspect allows for repeatability and gives science its relative objectivity.

Scion. In a plant graft, the part that is grafted on to the stock. The scion may be a bud or shoot.

Sclera. The tough outer protective opaque coat of the vertebrate eye. It consists of fibrous connective tissue, with the bundles running in all directions, and maintains the shape of the eye. It is continuous with the transparent cornea in front of the eye.

Sclereid. Any sclerenchyma cell, excluding the fibers. The various forms of sclereid include the star-shaped astrosclereid, the rod-shaped macro-sclereid, and the isodiametric stone cell.

Sclerenchyma. The main supporting tissue in plants, made up of cells with heavily thickened often lignified walls and empty lumina. Unlike collenchyma, it is not very extensible and is thus not formed in quantity until after the young tissues have fully differentiated. Sclerenchyma is often found associated with vascular tissue ad exists as two distinct types of cell; the fiber and the sclereid.

Scleroprotein. One of a group of proteins obtained from the exoskeletal structures of animals. They are insoluble in water, salt solutions, dilute acids, and alkalis. This group exhibits a wide range of both physical and chemical properties. Typical examples of scleroproteins are keratin (hair), elastin (elastic tissue), and collagen (connective tissue).

Sclerotium. The resting body of certain fungi, e.g. ergot, formed from a mass of hyphae.

Sclerotome. The part of each of the somites of vertebrates that contributes to the axial skeleton.

Scolex. The head of a cestode. It is spherical, with a narrow neck leading to the region where proglottids are produced. It has a crown of hooks and four lateral suckers for attaching the worm to the lining of the gut of the final host.

Scrotum. A pouch of skin that hangs external to the body directly behind the penis in most male mammals. It is divided into two compartments, eah containing a testis. The testes are thus maintained at a temperature lower than that of the body in order to insure optimum development of sperm.

Scutellum. The part of the embryo of Gramineae (grasses) that lies next to the endosperm. Some believe it to be the modified cotyledon while others think that the scutellum and coleoptile together represent the cotyledon.

Scyphistoma. The polyp stage in the life cycle of scyphozoans (jellyfish), which develops from the planula. It undergoes transverse splitting (strobilization) to produce small free-swimming ephyrae, which develop into adult jellyfish.

Sebaceous gland. A gland, situated at the upper end of a hair follicle, near the skin surface, that secretes an oily secretion, sebum, into the follicle. Sebum keeps hair and skin in good condition and has antiseptic properties.

Sebum. A complex oily secretion produced by the sebaceous glands in the mammalian skin. It is secreted onto the skin preventing desiccation, and onto the hairs and skin making them water-repellent. It also contains an antiseptic ingredient to kill bacteria.

Secondary plant body. The parts of the plant formed by secondary growth, e.g. secondary vascular tissue produced by ther intrafascicular cambium and cork cells produced by the phellogen.

Secondary structure. For proteins refers to that aspect of a proteins three dimensional structure which is due to the geometry of amino acid bonding between adjacent amino acids and short range hydrogen bonding. Typical secondary structures are pleated plates and alpha helices.

Second Law of Thermodynamics. The second law says that no process is 100% efficient because heat is always produced. Another way of stating this is that any process that does work produces heat. Still another way of stating this law is that in a closed system entropy tends to increase.

Secretin. A polypeptide hormone secreted by the mucosa of the duodenum and jejunum when the stomach empties its contents into the intestine. It stimulates alkaline pancreatic secretions to neutralize the acidic chyme from the stomach. Its secretion is also stimulated by the release of bile.

Secretion. Substances of fluids produced in cells and released to the surrounding medium. The secretion may be a fluid or molecules (e.g. enzymes, hormones). The term is also used for the process of producing the secretion.

Seed ferns. Seed-bearing plants represented only by fossil forms that flourished in the Carboniferous but became extinct in the Cretaceous. The plant body resembled a fern and did not produce flowers, the seeds developing from megasporangia borne on the fronds.

Segment. One of a series of repeated parts of the body.

Segmentation. An animal body plan in which the organism is subdivided into serially arranged units. Think of your back bone or even the bones in your hands as examples of segmentation.

Segregation. The separation of the two alleles of a gene into different gametes, brought about by the separation of homologous chromosomes during meiosis.

Seismonasty. (Seismonastic movements) A nastic movement in response to shock.

Selection pressure. The intensity with which the environment eliminates a particular phenotype, so causing the gene responsible for this to decrease in the population. It is thus a measure of the force of natural selection.

Selfish DNA. DNA that can move around within the genome of an organism or insert copies of itself at various sites without serving any apparent useful function. The prime examples of selfish DNA are the mobile genetic elements called transposons.

Some biologist also regard introns a selfish DNA.

Self assembly. The concept that certain molecules can organize themselves spontaneously into more complex forms. The organization of protein folding and the phospholipid bilayer are prime examples.

Selfish behavior. Behavior that increases the organism's ability to survive and leave offspring while at best only incidentally benefiting other members of the same species.

Self-sterility. The condition in many hermaphrodite animals and plants whereby male gametes cannot fertilize female gametes from the same individual.

Seliwanoff's test. A standard test for the presence of fructose in solution. A few drops of Seliwanoff's reagent, resorcinol in hydrochloric acid, are heated with the test solution. A red color or red precipitate indicates fructose.

Semen. A fluid containing spermatozoa and nutritive substances, produced by male mammals. The testes produce the spermatozoa, and the other constituents of the semen are produced by the prostate gland and the seminal vesicles. Semin is placed in the body of the female during mating.

Semi-conservative replication. Refers to the fact that each daughter molecule produced when DNA replicates has one of the original parent strands and one newly constructed strand.

Seminiferous tubule. A mass of minute coiled tubules within the vertebrate testis in which spermatozoa are produced. In man, each is about 15 mm in diameter and 50 cm long and drains into small collecting ducts.

Semi-permeable (selectively permeable). refers to a membrane that will let some material through and other other material.

Sensory neuron. A neuron leading from a sensory receptor to the central nervous system and sending information from the receptor to the central nervous system. Sensory neurons may either link to a receptor or itself be a receptor at one end, as in some pain receptors.

Sensitization. The increase in the reaction of an organism or cell to an antigen to which it has been previously exposed. It may occur naturally or be artificially induced, e.g. following vaccination.

Sepal. One of the structures situated immediately below the petals of a flower. Their collective name is the calyx. They are often green and hairy and enclose and protect the flower bud. Sometimes they are brightly colored and atttract insects for pollination.

Septum. A wall, partition, or membrane separating two cavities. For example a septum separates the coelom of one segment of an earthworm from that of the next segment; the capsule of a poppy is divided by septa.

Sex limited. An aspect of the organism's phenotype that is only or usually expressed by one sex. For example pattern baldness runs in families but the women usually will not express it even if they have the correct genotype. Its typically only expressed in the males. Contrast sex linked.

Sex linked. Sex linked traits are traits that are due to alleles found on the X chromosome. Thus color blindness is a recessive sex linked trait because if the male has an allele for color blindness it will be expressed in that male since he does not have another X chromosome potentially carried the dominant allele for normal vision. Note carefully that females can be color blind if they are homozygous recessive. If color blindness was really sex limited, it would restricted, say to males, regardless of the female's genotype with respect to color blindness.

Shared homologue. A character found in two or more taxa whose most recent common ancestor also had (or can be inferred to have had) it.

Shell. With reference to electrons the shell is an energy level. Roughly, the further the electrons are from the nucleus of the atom the more energy they have. Chemical properties of an atom are determined by the number of electrons in the outermost shell.

Short-germ. Mode of DEVELOPMENT in some lower insect groups (e.g. Orthoptera) in which only the most anterior head structures are defined before or during gastrulation.

Sieve area. Area of sieve element wall containing clusters of pores through which protoplasts of adjacent sieve elements are connected.

Sieve plate. End-wall of SIEVE TUBE MEMBER, where pores are larger than in lateral sieve area; highly differentiated.

Sieve tube. Series of SIEVE TUBE MEMBERS, arranged end-to-end and interconnected by SIEVE PLATES. Functions in transport of food materials (e.g. surcose, amino acids). Lacking nuclei at maturity.

Sign stimulus. A stimulus from the environment, especially from another organism, that causes an organism to exhibit a stereotyped set of instinctive behaviors. Often called a releaser.

Sinus venosus. Chamber of vertebrate HEART, between veins and auricle(s). Thin-walled; absent from adult birds and mammals.

Siphonaceous. Coenocytic; e.g. members of several orders of algae, which are filamentous, sac-like or tubular, without cross-walls.

Siphonophora. These creatures are a group of organisms related to jellyfish, coral and sea anemones. While they superficially resemble jellyfish, each apparent organism is really a complex colony of multicellular organisms called polyps. The polyps each have their own specific function in the colony but are genetically identical to each other.

Siphonostele. Type of STELE containing hollow cylinder of vascular tissue surrounding a pith.

Sirenia. Order of placental mammals. Manatees, dugongs (seacows). Aquantic (coastal and river-dwelling) and herbivorous, with trasversely expanded tail, front legs modified as fippers and vestigial hindlegs. One pair of mammary glands. Not closely related to cetaceans.

Skeleton. Any compoent of an animal's anatomy serving

for muscle attachment and/ or transmission of restoring forces extending a contracted muscle.

Skotophile. Literally, dark-loving, darkreceptive phase of circadian rhythms, lasting about 12 hours.

Skull. The skeleton of the head. In mammals it consists of a cranium enclosing the brain and the bones of the face and jaw. All the joints between the individual bones of the skull are immovable except for the joint between the mandible and the rest of the skull. There is a large opening at the base of the skull through which the spinal cord passes from the brain.

Slow virus. Any of a group of quasiviral or subviral agents formerly thought to be responsible for the diseases scrapie in sheep and bovine spongiform encephalopathy in cattle. Thee diseases are now generally regarded as being caused by abnormal prion proteins.

Small intestine. The portion of the *alimentary canal between the stomach and the large intestine. It is subdivided into the *duodenum, *jejunum, and *ileum. It plays an essential role in the final digestion and absorption of food.

Smuts. Members of the only order (Ustilaginales) within thr fungal class Ustomycetes (Division BASIDIOMYCOTA). Important plant pathogens, often of their flowers, producing masses of black, sooty spores.

Smooth endoplasmic reticulum (Smooth ER). A series of membranous networks involved in the final modification of proteins and the synthesis of lipids. Contrast **rough ER**.

SnoRNAs (small nucleolar RNAs). A group of eukaryotic non-coding RNAs directing 2-0-ribose methylation and pseudouridylation of rRNA, tRNA and ncRNAs, forming base pairs with sequences close to the site to be modified.

Social behavior. Behavior involving interactions with other members of the same species. There are different degrees of such interaction, thus even "solitary" animals such as tigers will exhibit at least some degree of social behavior, if only during mating.

Sociobiology. The branch of biology that studies the evolutionary basis of social behavior.

Sodium. Symbol Na. A soft silvery element that is a major essential element required by animals. It is important in maintaining the acidbase balance and in controlling the volume of extracellular fluid and functions in the transmission of nerve impulses.

Sodium chloride. A colourless crystalline solid. NaCl, that is soluble in water. Sodium chloride has a key role in biological systems in maintaining electrolyte balances, It is used as a food preservative.

Sodium fluoride. A crystalline compound NaF. It is highly toxic but in very dilute solution it is used in the fluoridation of water for the prevention of tooth decay on account of its ability to replace OH groups with F groups in the material of dental enamel.

Soil erosion. The removal and thining of the soil layer due to climatic and physical processes, such is highly rainfall, which is greatly accelerated by certain human activities, such as deforestation. Soil erosion can lead to a loss agricultural land and if unchecked, eventually results in desertification.

Sol. A mixture involving a solvent such as water and very large molecules or groups of molecules that are mixed into the solvent. The large groups of molecules are prevented from settling out by a combination of hydration shells and kinetic energy from the water molecules. A change in pH can cause these large molecules to settle out and not be available to the cell. A **gel** is similar but the molecules are in a mesh work which holds the solvent molecules in place. Think "Jello".

Solute potential. The component of water potential that is due to the presence of solute mollecules. It always has a negative value as solutes lower the water potential of the system.

Somatic. Refers to body. For instance, somatic cells refers to all the cells in the body except for the germ cells.

Somatic nervous system. That part of the peripheral nervous system which is under voluntary control..ok more or less under voluntary control. **Contrast autonomic nervous system.**

Solvent. A substance, usually a liquid or gas into which another substance will dissolve. The substance being dissolved is the **solute** and the two substances together is the **solution**. Obviously, such as in the cell solutions may be a mixture of many solutes in the solvent water. We are interested in these three terms because cells often operate at particular concentrations of solutes and water.

Somite. Any of a series of segmented blocks of tissue in animal embryos that develop from the mesoderm. In vertebrate embryos they lie on the dorsal side of the notochord and give rise to the vertebral column, ribs, dermis, and striated muscle. In invertebrates showing metameric segmentation the somites give rise to the body segments.

Sonicator. A device used to break down cells using ultrasonic waves. Ultrasonic metal red, which is placed in a suspension of the cells. The vibrations cause the plasma membranes to rupture and the cellular contents are released into the surrounding medium.

Soredium. A small body, consisting of a core of algal cells surrounded by fungal hyphae, that functions as a structure of vegetative propagation ion lichens.

Sorosis. A type of composite fruit formed from an entire inflorescence spike. Mulberry and pineapple fruits are examples.

Sorus. 1. Any of the spore-producing structures on the undersurface of a fern frond, visible as rows of small brown dots. 2. A reproductive area on the thallus of some algae, e.g. Laminaria. 3. Any of various spore producing structures in certain fungi.

Spadix. A flowering shoot (a type of spike) with a large fleshy floral axis bearing small, usually unisexual, flowers. It is protected by a large petal-like bract, the spathe, and is characteristic of plants of the family Araceae (e.g. calla lily).

Spatial learning. The ability of organisms learn relationships and perhaps solve problems in two or three dimensional space. Examples of this type of learning involve the navigational abilities of bees and birds as well as our abilities to get around in large cities.

Specialization Increasing adaptation of an organism to a particular environment.

Speciation. The evolutionary processes by which new kinds of organisms evolve from preexisting kinds or evolve from currently existing kinds.

Species. In biology a species generally taken to be either the lowest level of taxonomic classification or a group of interbreeding individuals that are reproductively isolated from other organisms. A species in biology is not a "kind" in Plato's sense of the word.

Species isolating mechanisms. Diverging behaviors, physical attributes, or habitat preferences found in closely related species that have the effect of preventing mating and or the production of offspring. Species isolating mechanism may be prezygotic or post zygotic. Pre-mating or post mating.

Spectroscopy. The study of methods of producing and analysing spectra using spectroscopes and other instruments. Spectroscopy is employed in a wide range of biological research areas, such as biochemistry and toxicology, for the identification of metabolites and other compounds of biological significance.

Spermatheca. A sac or receptacle in some female or hermaphrodite animals (e.g. earthworms) in which sperm from the mate is stored until the eggs are ready to be fertilized.

Spermatid. A nonmotile cell, produced during spermatogenesis, that subsequently differentiates into a mature spermatozoon. Four spermatids are formed after two meiotic divisions of a primary spermatocyte and therefore contain in haploid number of chromosomes.

Spermatium. A type of non-motile male sex cell that is produced by the red algae and by certain fungi (e.g. the rusts).

Spermatocyte. A diploid cell in the testis that divides by meiosis to give rise to four spermatids. A primary spermatocyte develops from a spermatogonium. Two secondary spermatocytes result from the first meiotic division of a primary spermatocyte; each of these products two spermatids after the second meiotic division.

Spermatogonium. Any of the diploid cells in the walls of the seminiferous tubules of the testis that give rise to the primary spermatocytes.

Spermatophyta. In traditional classifications, a division of the plant kingdom containing plants that reproduce by means of seeds. In modern systems seed plants are grouped into separate phyla, the most important of which are the Anthophyta and Coniferophyta.

Spherosome. A small spherical organelle found in the cytoplasm of plant cells. Up to 1 mm in diameter and bounded by a single membrane, it synthesizes and stores lipids.

Sphincter. A ring of smooth muscle that can close off a tubular structure such as an arteriole or part of the colon.

Spike. A type of recemose inflorescence in which stalkless flowers arise from a undivided floral axis, as in plantain and Orchis. In the family Gramineae the flowers are grouped in clusters called spikelets, which may be arranged to form a compound spike (as in wheat).

Spinal nerves. Pairs of nerves that arise from the spinal cord. In humans there are 31 pairs. Each nerve arises from a dorsal root and a ventral root and contains both motor and sensory fibres. The spinal nerves form an important part of the peripheral nervous system.

Spindle. In mitosis and meiosis the **microtubule** assembly to which the chromosomes become attached.

Spine. A hard pointed protective structure on a plant that is formed thrugh modification of a leaf, part of a leaf, or a stipule. The edge of the holly leaf is drawn out into spines, but in cacti the whole leaf is modified as a spine.

Spinocerebellar tracts. Pathways of neurons that transfer sensory information from the spinal cord to the cerebellum of the brain.

Spirillum. Any rigid spiral-shaped bacterium. Generally, spirilla are Gram-negative, aerobic, and highly motile, bearing flagella either in tufts or singly. They occur in soil and water, feeding on organic matter.

Spleen. A vertebrate organ, lying behind the stomach, that is basically a collection of lymphoid tissue. Its functions include producing lymphocytes and destroying foreign particles. It actsas a reservoir for erythrocytes and can regulate the number in circulation. It is also the site for the breakdown of wornout erythrocytes end it stores the iron they contain.

Sporangiophore. The simple or branched stalk that bears one or more sporangia.

Spore. A resistant single cell. In plants the spores are products of meiosis produced on special leaves called **sporophylls.** The plant bearing the sporophylls is called the **sporophyte**. **Spores** that land in suitable habitat germinate and develop in Haploid plants called **gametophytes**.

Spore mother cell. A diploid cell that gives rise to four haploid spores by meiosis.

Sporogonium. The sporophyte generation in mosses and liverworts. It is made up of an absorptive foot, a stalk (seta), and a spore-producing capsule. It may be completely or patially dependent on the gametophyte.

Sporophore. The aerial spore-producing part of certain fungi; for example, the stalk and cap of a mushroom.

Sporophyte. In plants, a multicellular stage that produces haploid spores by meiosis. What we think of as a plant in everyday speech refers to the sporophyte stage of the plant life cycle.

Sport. An individual organisms that shows the effects of a mutation. The term is usually applied to atypical forms of plants in horticulture.

Squalene. An intermediate compound formed in the synthesis of cholesterol; it is a hydrocarbon containing 30 carbon atoms. The immediate oxidation of squalene to squalene 2,3-epoxide is the last common step in the synthesis of sterols in animals, plants , and fungi.

Squamous epithelium. A type of epithelium that is made up of flattened cells and therefore presents a small distance over which substances have to pass. This type of epithelium is found lining the alveoli in the lungs and Bowman's capsule in the kidney.

Stamen. The part of the flower that produces pollen. Basically a micro (or small) sporophyll. The stamen part where the pollen. grains develop is the **anther**. The narrow stalk supporting the anther is the **filament**.

Staminode. A sterile stamen. It may be rudimentary, consisting of only the flament, as an figwort, or it may form a conspicuous part of the flower, as in iris.

Standing crop. The nutritional portion of the biomass in an area at a given moment.

Stapes. The stirrup-shaped bone attached to the oval window of the ear, which forms the innermost ear ossicle in mammals. It is homologous with the hyomandibular of fishes.

Staphylococcus. A genus of Gram-positive spherical nonmotile bacteria. They are facultative anaerobes and do not form spores. Many species are parasites or pathogens of animals and some cause wound infections, abscesses, and a type of food poisoning. They are killed by pasteurization and many common disinfectants.

Starch. Any one of a number of polysaccharides produced by plants and other photosynthetic organisms as a means of storing excess carbohydrate. For example the white part of a potato consists of grains of starch stored in a specialized ground tissue. When the energy in the starch is needed by the plant, it is broken down to sucrose for transport and when the sucrose reaches the cells where it is needed it is converted to glucose and or fructose.

Starch sheath. The innermost layer of cells of the cortex replacing the endodermis in some stems, especially young herbaceous dicotyledonous stems. The starch sheath contains prominent starch grains and is thought by some to be involved in the perception of gravity.

Starch-statolith hypothesis. A hypothesis concerning the mechanism of gravity perception in plants.

Statoblast. An internal bud produced asexually by freshwater bryozoans. Statoblasts have a thick protective covering, enabling them to survive extremes of drought and temperature after they have broken away from the parent colony.

Statocyst. An organ concerned with the perception of gravity in invertebrates. Statocysts are seen, for example, in the tentacles of Obelia and in the antennules of the crawfish. It is similar in structure and function to the macula of vertebrates.

Statocyte. A plant cell containing statoliths, and thought to be involved in the perception of gravity.

Statolith. One of a number of large starch grains found in the statocytes, plant cells that are thought to be gravity sensitive. They most through the cytoplasm to the lowermost cell surface, enabling the platto detect the direction of gravity.

Stearic acid. A saturated carboxylic acid, which is widely distrubuted in nature as the glyceride ester. It is present in most fats and oils of animal and vegetable origin, particularly the socalled hard fats, i.e. those of higher melting point.

Stem cell. Any cell that remains undifferentiated and capable of unlimited division in order to provide new cells for growth or replacement of tissues. After division it may produce more stem cells or cells that differentiate into specialized tissue cells.

Stenohaline. Describing organisms that are unable to tolerate wide variations of salt concentrations in the environment.

Sterigma. A finger-like projection upon which spores are formed in many fungi. In basidiomycete fungi, four sterigmata, each bearing one basidiospore, are usually borne on each basidium. In certain ascomycete fungi, e.g. Penicillium, the sterigmata give rise to chains of conidiophores.

Steroid. A class of lipids characterized by a four carbon ring structure. Male hormones(androgens) and female hormones(estrogens) are steroids as is cholesterol. Cholesterol is an important component in cell membranes, increasing the flexibility of the membrane.

Sterol. A steroid with long aliphatic side chains and at least one hydroxyl group. They are lipid-soluble and often occur in membranes (e.g. cholesterol and ergosterol).

Stigma. The part of the pistil that receives the pollen grain.

Stilt root. An enlarged form of prop root, seen in some mangroves, that helps support plants in unstable soils.

Stimulus. A change in the external or internal environment of an organism that elicits a response in the organism. The stimulus does not provide the energy for the response.

Stipe. 1. In the more highly differentiated algae (e.g. wracks and kelps), the stalk between the holdfast and the blade.

2. The stalk of the fruiting body of certain basidiomycete fungi (e.g. Agaricus) that bears the cap or pileus.

Stipule. A modified leaf found as an outgrowth from the petiole or leaf base. Stipules are seen around the base of the petiole in the garden pea, in which they serve as additional photosynthetic organs, and growing along the length of the petiole in the rose.

Stoma. In plants, the small pores located usually on the lower surface of leaves through which gas exchange and transpiration takes place.

Stomium. A structure involved in the dispersal of spores in certain plant structures. For example in the sporangium of the fern Dryopteris the stomium is seen below the annulus and is gradually ruptured as the annulus drives out. In the stamen of angiosperms the cells in the groove between the two pollen sacs form a stomium, and rupture as the anther dries out.

Stomodaeum. An invagination of ectoderm of the animal embryo that forms the anterior region of the alimentary canal the mouth, pharynx, and esophagus in mammals.

Stone cell. An isodiametric sclereid found either singly or in groups in the parenchyma and phloem of stems and some fruits (e.g. pear).

Stroma. The region inside the chloroplast, outside the **grana**, where the **Calvin-Benson cycle** of photosynthesis takes place.

Style. The elongated part of the pistil just below the stigma.

Subarachnoid space. The space between the middle arachnoid membrane and the inner pia mater, which surrounds and protects the brain and spinal cord in vertebrates. It is crossed by delicate tissue strands and filled with cerebrospinal fluid, which cushions the central nervous system against external shocks.

Subclavian artery. In mammals, a large paired artery that carries oxygenated blood to the forelimbs. It arises on the left side from the aorta and on the right side from the innominate artery.

Subcutaneous tissue. A layer of tissue beneath the dermis, which contains stored fat. It is important in restricting heat loss in aquatic mammals and in some hibernating mammals, in the latter it also acts as an essential food store.

Suberin. A mixture of substances produced in the walls of cork tissue. It is similar in properties and functions to cutin. The Casparian band in roots and some stems contains suberin, lignin, or similar substances.

Subhymenium. The intermediate layer of tissue between the trama and hymenium in the gills of basidiomycete fungi.

Subspecies. The taxonomic group below the species level. Crosses can generally be made between subspecies of a given species but this may be prevented in the wild by various isolating mechanisms, e.g. geographical isolation or different flowerring times.

Substrate. In biochemistry, the substances being acted up by an enzyme.

Surface tension. The tendency of water to behave is if it is covered by a semirigid film.

Suspension. A mixture of a liquid and small particles that stay in the liquid rather than settling out because of kinetic energy of the solvent's molecules. Milk is a good example of a suspension. The cytoplasm of the cell is, at least in part, a suspension of various particles.

Symbiosis. The living together in close association of two or more species. In some parts of the world symbiosis is used solely referring to a beneficial relationship, but the modern meaning is much broader.

Sympatric speciation. The process by which new species evolve within the range of its parent species without any sort of geographical isolation. This type of speciation is well documented in plants where it typically involves polyploidy. Circumstantial evidence suggests that this mode of speciation may be important in certain groups of animals as well.

Syrinx. The soundproducing organ in birds. It is similar to the vocal cords but positioned at the base of the trachea.

Systole. The phase of the heartbeat cycle when the cardiac muscle contractes. Contraction of the atria propels blood into the ventricles; contraction of the ventricles expels blood into the aorta and pulmonary artery.

T

Taxis. A taxis is behavior consisting of a directed movement of the whole organism toward or away from a stimulus.

Taxon. A group of any rank in taxonomy. Ranunculaceae and Triticum (a genus) are examples.

Taxonomy. In biology, the science dealing with the classification and identification of organisms.

Tectum. The dorsal roof region of the midbrain that is the dominant brain center in fishes and amphibians. It is also important in reptiles and birds and gives rise to a pair of prominent optic lobes. In mammals the rectum is much lobes. In mammals the tectum is much less important, being concerned only with certain visual and auditory reflexes.

Telomere. A region at the tip of a chromosome or chromatid that consists of repeating sequences of nucleotide bases. Telomeres are important because as chromosomes replicate, the telomere shrinks in size. In some cells and organisms the telomere is restored to its original length by an enzyme called telomerase. If a particular cell does not have telomerase, the cell can only undergo a set number of cell divisions until dying out. Scientists believe this process is related to the aging process of multicellular organisms including humans.

Telophase. The final stage in mitosis and meiosis before cells enter interphase. During this stage chromosomes uncoil and disperse, the nuclear spindle degenerates, and a new nuclear membrane forms. The cytoplasm may also divide during this phase.

Telson. The last segment of the abdomen of crustaceans, flattened to form a plate . In the lobster, the telson and the uropods form a fan that can be used for swimming backwards for short distances.

Temperate phage. A bacteriophage that becomes integrated into the bacterial DNA and multiples with it, rather than, replicating independently and causing lysis of the bacterium.

Temperature. Temperature is really a way of measuring the average kinetic energy of all the molecules or atoms of the substance being studied. Temperature differs from heat in that heat is the total amount of kinetic energy in the substance being studied. For instance, two rooms may both be at 27 degrees Celsius, but if the second room has twice the volume, the room will contain twice the heat of the first room.

Tendinous cords. Tough strands of connective tissue that run from the undersides of the bicuspid and tricuspid valves to muscles in the walls of the left and right ventricles of the heart respectively. They prevent the valves from turning inside out under pressure of ventricular contraction.

Tendon. The tough nonelastic connective tissue that joins a muscle to a borne. It consists of a mass of parallel white collagen fibres, which are continuous with those of the muscle sheath and the periosteum of the bone. When the muscle contracts, the tendon pulls on the bone, causing movement at the joint.

Tergum. The plate, stiffened by chitin, that forms the protective dorsal covering to each segment of the thorax and abdomen of an insect.

Terminalization. The movement of chiasmata to the end of he bivalent arms, a process that may occur during late prophase I of meiosis. The chiasmata can slip off the ends of the bivalents, and thus chiasma frequency may be reduced by terminalization.

Tertiary Structure. In proteins, the three dimensional folding of the protein due to hydrophobic and hydrophilic interactions with water. The protein chain's primary and secondary structure folds into a complex three dimensional shape. This shape is sensitive to the charge environment of the solution. A change in pH can, for instance, alter the shape of an enzyme activating it or rendering it inactive.

Territory. An area containing a resource that is actively defended by an animal from other animals be they of the same species or in some cases of different species. Note that a territory is not the same thing as a home range in that a home range is where the animal may tend to roam.

Testa. The hard dry protective covering of a seed, formed from the integuments of the ovule. After fertilization the layers of the integuments fuse and become thickened and pigmented. In some species the testa may be modified in some way, as in Gossypium in which long cotton fibres develop on the seed coat surface.

Test cross. A mating designed to tell if an organism with the dominant phenotype is homozygous or heterozygous (carrying a recessive allele). This is done by mating the individual with a homozygous recessive individual. Of course, this isn't often practical and today for many genetic systems there are biochemical tests which eliminate the need for test crosses.

Tetrad. A group of four chromatids formed by the association of a pair of homologous chromosomes during prophase I of meiosis.

Tetrapod. A vertebrate with four limbs, i.e. an amphibian, bird, mammal, or reptile.

Thalamus. A part of the midbrain that relays sensory and motor impulses to and from the appropriate centres in the cerebral hemispheres.

Thallus. A simple plant body showing no differentiation into root, leaf, and stem and lacking a true vascular system. It may be unior multicellular, and is found in the algae, lichens, bryophytes, and the gametophyte generation of the pteridophytes.

Thermonasty. A nastic movement in response to change in temperature.

Theory. A complex set of well tested assumptions, well tested hypothesis which guides the research within a particular area of science, leading to new hypothesis and predictions within that area of science. Examples of theories include the theories of relativity, quantum mechanics in physics, and the theory of evolution in biology.

Thermophile. An organism that thrives at temperatures above those where life normally can be found. Usually 50 degrees Celsius or above. Some thermophiles in hot springs and in deep sea thermal vents live at near the boiling point of water.

Thigmotropism. An orientation toward or away from a touch stimulus. Found in the tendrils of many vines.

Thoracic duct. A dorsal longitudinal lymphatic vessel-the major vessel of the lymphatic system-that collects lymph from most of the body. In mammals, it begins below the diaphragm, ascends in front of the vertebral column, and drains into the innominate vein at the base of the neck.

Thoracic vertebrae. The vertebrae of the upper back region, there are 12 in humans. Each is distinguished by articular surfaces on the sides of the body and on the transverse processes for the upper ends of a pair of ribs.

Thorn. A stiff sharply pointed woody process that may be found on the stems of vascular plants. It is a modified branch and is supplied with vascular tissue.

Threshold. The electrical potential across a neuron cell membrane that is just sufficient to trigger an action potential.

Thrombin. An enzyme that converts the soluble protein fibrinogen into the fibrous fibrin during blood clotting. It is formed from prothrombin under the influence of thromboplastin, calcium ions, and other clotting factors, which are activated when blood is removed from the circulation, usually by injury.

Thylakoid. A flattened membranous sac that comprises part of the granum in a chloroplast. The pigment systems and electron transport systems for the light dependent reactions of photosynthesis are part of the thylakoid membrane.

Thymine. A nitrogenous base found in DNA. It has a pyrimidine ring structure.

Thyroid gland. A gland situated in the neck, consisting of two lateral lobes on either side of the trachea ad larynx, giving the gland a butterfly appearance. Its main function is the regulation of metabolic rate by production of thyroid hormones.

Thyroid hormones. Hormones produced by the thyroid gland, which increase cell metabolism. The most important is thyroxine.

Tissue. A group of similar cells bound together by intercellular material that carry out a common set of functions.

Titre. Usually, a relative measure of the amount of antibody in a fluid, usually serum, The greatest dilution capable of producing a particular detectable antibodyantigen reaction is its titre. This assay technique can be used to compare titres in different samples.

T Lymphocyte. Cells that form the basis of the cell mediated part of the immune system. These cells do not respond to free antigens in the blood stream and do not produce antibodies.

Toadstool. Common name for fruiting bodies of fungi belonging to the Agaricaceae. Often wrongly assumed that all are poisonous, although some are.

Tonic receptor. Slow-adapting RECEPTOR, continuing to respond with action potentials throughout unchanging stimulus. Conveys information about the duration of a stimulus.

Tonoplast. The membrane that surrounds the VACUOLE in plant cells. It plays an important role in the active transport of certain ions into the vacuole, and their retention there.

Tornaria. Ciliated planktonic larval stage of the HEMICHORDATA. Its development by radial cleavage and ENTEROCOELY suggests links with echinoderms.

Totipotency. The inherent capability of a single cell to provide the genetic programme required to direct the development of an entire individual.

Toxoid. Toxin modified so as to retain its antigenicity but to lose its toxicity. Used in VACCINES against human diphtheria and tetanus.

Trace. Term sometimes used for an isotopic label.

Trachea. In vertebrates, the tube leading from the pharynx into the thorax where it branches to form the primary bronchi into the lungs. In insects and many other arthropods one of the air tubes that forms part of the insect respiratory system.

Tracheary element. General term for the water-conducting cell in vascular plants.

Trans acting control elements. Regulatory genetic elements whose products are not limited in their binding to the DNA molecule of which they form a part.

Transactivation. Interaction of steroid receptors with TRANSACTING CONTROL ELEMENTS on DNA to stimulate transcription of hormonally responsive genes.

Transamination. Transfer by a transaminase of a amino group from an amino acid, to a keto acid, producing respectively a keto acid and an amino acid.

Transcriptome. The collection of genes expressed, or transcribed, from genomic DNA by a cell. Unlike the genome, it is highly dynamic. And changes in multigene expression patterns give us clues about regularly mechanisms and the biochemical pathways involved in cellular functions.

Transfection. In prokaryotes, reserved for the uptake by transformation of naked phage DNA to produce a bacteriophage infection.

Transferase. Enzyme transferring a nonhydrogen functional group from one molecule to another.

Transfer efficiency. The efficiency with which energy is passed through various steps in the trophic structure of a COMMUNITY.

Transformation. The incorporation of naked DNA into the cells of bacteria causing an alteration in the bacteria cell's phenotype.

Transgene. Any gene introduced by GENE MANIPULATION from one organism into an organism of a different species.

Transition. Any error in DNA replication during which one pyrimidine nucleotide is inserted in lieu of another, or one purine nucleotide in lieu of another.

Translation threshold. The basic reproductive rate of a parasite that is a necessary condition for a disease to spread.

Translation. The process of taking the sequence of nucleotide triplets(codons) in a strand of messenger RNA and using that sequence to make a polypeptide.

Translocation. The movement of organic compounds , especially sucrose, through a plant by means of the phloem tissue.

Transpiration. Water loss by evaporation from a plant, especially through the stomates on the leaves.

Transport Proteins. Proteins found in the membranes of cells and organelles that are responsible for the movement of many substances into the cell or to the outside of the cell. Sometimes these proteins are passive gateways for substances to diffuse into or out of the cell. Other transport proteins use energy to actively pump molecules into the cell or to the outside.

Transposon. A segment of DNA capable of shifting from one position in the eukaryote genome to another. Often transposons code for enzymes that facilitate the transposon's movement. Sometimes called "jumping genes".

Transcription. The process of making an RNA molecule based on a sequence of DNA nucleotide bases.

Transducer. A structure, mechanical or biological that translates one form of energy into electrical energy. For instance the rods and cones in the eye are transducers that translate light into electrical energy.

Transfer RNA(tRNA). A type of RNA that carries an amino acid at its back end and has the so called anticodon at its front end to complement the messenger RNA codons in translation.

Transverse division. Cell division in the plane of the long axis of a plant (or plant organ).

Transverse process. Lateral projection one on each side, of neural arch of tetrapod vertebra, with which the head of the rib articulates.

Transverse section. Section cut perpendicular to longitudinal axis of an organism.

Transversion. Any error in DNA replication during which a purine nucleotide is subsituted for a pyrimidine, or vice versa.

Trentepohliophyceae. This is a small class, with one order and four genera, in the algal division CHLOROPHYTA, Species of Trentepohlia grow on rocks or tree trunks or leaves.

Tribe. Taxonomic category between subfamily and genus, used to indicate a group of closely related genera. Tribe names normally endeae in botany and ini in zoology.

Triglyceride. A lipid synthesized from one glycerol and three fatty acid molecules. Includes what we call animal fats and vegetable oils.

Triploblastic. Animals with a body organization derived from three GERM LAYERS. Includes all metazoans except coelenterates, which are diploblastic.

Triploid. Nuclei, cells or organisms with three times the haploid number of chromosomes. A form of POLYPLOIDY. Triploid individuals are usually sterile due to failure of chromosomes to pair up during meiosis.

Trisomy. Nucleus, cell or organism where one chromosome pair is represented by three chromosomes, giving a chromosome complement of zn+1. May result from NONDISJUNCTION.

Trochanter. 1. Any knob for muscle attachment on the vertebrate femur. Three occur on mammalian femurs, largest in humans being conspicuous at hip joint. 2. Segment lying second from base of an insect leg.

Trophic structure. The organization of a COMMUNITY described in terms of energy flow through its various trophic levels.

Tropism. A tropism is behavior consisting of an orientation toward or away from a stimulus. In contrast to a taxis, tropisms do not involve movement of the whole organism relative to the stimulus.

True predator. A predator that kills other organisms more or less immediately after attacking them, killing several or many over the course of its lifetime.

Truffle. Fungal genus that produces a subterranean fruting body; prized as a gastronomic delicacy.

Trumpet hyphae. Drawn out sieve cells, wider at the crosswalls than in the middle, in some brown algae. Active transport of photosynthates through sieve cells occurs in this Order.

Trypsin. Protease enzyme secreted in its inactive form by vertebrate pancreas and converted to active form by ENTEROKINASE.

Tryptophan. An aromatic AMIND ACID, essential in the human diet end, like phenylalanine and tyrosine, a product of phosphoenlopyruvate and erythrose 4-phosphate addition, with subsequent derivation, in bacteria and plants.

Tsetse fly. Genus of dipteran fly, sucking vertebrate blood and acting as vector for trypanosomes.

Tuber. Swollen end of RHIZOME, bearing buds in axils of scale-like rudimentary leaves, e.g. potato; or swollen root, e.g. dahlia. Tubers contain stored food materials and are organs of vegetative propagation.

Tumour. Swelling caused by uncontrolled growth of cells; may be malignant or benign.

Tunica corpus. Organization of shoot of most flowering plants and a few gymnophytes, comprising one or more peripheral layers of cells and an interior. Tunica layers undergo surface growth and corpus undergoes volume growth.

Tupaiidae. The family of modern tree shrews.

Turbellaria. Class of PLATYHELMINTHES. Mostly aquatic and free-living. Epidermis ciliated, especially ventrolaterally, for locomotion. Gut a simple or branched enteron, with ventral mouth and protrusible pharynx.

Turbidity. Level of cloudiness of a suspension, commonly of cells. Often used as indicator of density of cells in suspension.

Turion. Detached winter bud by means of which many aquatic plants survive the winter; e.g. Myriphyllum.

U

Ubiquinone. Any of a group of related quinone-derived compounds that serve as electron carriers in the electron transport chain reactions of cellular respiration. Ubiquinone molecules have side chains of different lengths in different types of organisms but function in similar ways.

Ulna. The larger of the two bones in the forearm of vertebrates. It articulates with the outer carpals at the wrist and with the humerus at the elbow.

Ultracentrifuge. A high-speed centrifuge used to measure the rate of sedimentation of colloidal particles or to separate macromolecules, such as proteins or nucleic acids, from solutions. Ultracentrifuges are electrically driven and are capable of speeds up to 60000 rpm.

Ultradian rhythm. A biological thythm whose periodicity is greater than a day. For example, the body temperature of hibernating animals often shows periodic transient increases corresponding to brief period of arousal. Also, the reproductive behaviour of many animals follows a circalunar rhythm linked to the 29.5-day lunar cycle.

Ultrafiltration. The process in which hydrostatic pressure causes water and small dissolved molecules and ions to move across a membrane against a concentration gradient. Ultrafiltration is responsible for the formation of tissue fluid and glomerular filtrate from blood. In both these processes the ultrafiltered fluid has the same composition as the plasma except that it does not contain blood cells or large protein molecules.

Ultrasonics. The study and use of pressure waves that have a frequency in excess of

20000 Hz and are therefore inaudible to the human ear. Ultrasound is used in medical diagnosis, particularly in conditions such as pregnancy, in which X-rays could have a harmful effect.

Ultrastructure. The submicroscopic, almost molecular, structure of living cells, which is revealed by the use of a electron microscope.

Umbel. A type of racemose inflorescence in which stalked flowers arise from the same point on the flower axis, resembling the spokes of an umbrella. An involucre of bracts may occur at the point where the stalks emerge. This arrangement is characteristic of the family Umbelliferae in which the inflorescence is usually a compound umbel.

Umbilical cord. The cord that connects the embryo to the placenta in mammals. It contains a vein and two arteries that carry blood between the embryo and placenta. It is severed after birth to free the newly born animal from the placenta, and shrivels to leave a scar, the navel, on the animal.

Uniformitarianism. An important assumption in science that says that the physical laws that operate today have operated in the same manner in earlier times, back to close to the beginning of the universe. It does not mean that conditions have been unchanging in past times.

Ungulate. A herbivorous mammal with hoofed feet. Ungulates are grouped into two orders. Artiodactyla and Perissodactyla.

Unguligrade. Describing the gait of ungulates, in which only the tips of the digits are on the ground and the rest of the foot is off the ground.

Unicellular. Describing tissues, organs, or organisms consisting of a single cell. For example, the reproductive organs of some algae and fungi are unicellular. Unicellular organisms include bacteria, protozoans, and certain fungi and algae.

Unipolar neuron. A neuron that has one main process, the axon, extending from its cell body. Unipolar neurons include many sensory neurons and many vertebrate motor neurons and interneurons.

Uniporter. A transport protein that moves molecules across a membrane in one direction only down their concentration gradient.

Uniramia. In some classifications, a phylum of arthropods that contains the classes Chilopoda, Diplopoda, Pauropoda and Symphyla, and Hexapoda. Members are characterized by uniramous appendages.

Uniramous appendage. A type of appendage that is characteristic of insects and other members of the Uniramia. It consists of an unbranched series of segments.

Unisexual. Describing animals or plants with either male or female reproductive organs but not both. Most of the more advanced animals are unisexual but plants are often hermaphrodite. Flowers that contain either stamens or carpels but not both are also described as unisexual.

Unit. A specified measure of a physical quantity, such as length, mass, time, etc., specified multiples of which are used to express magnitudes of that physical quantity. For scientific purposes previous systems of units have now been replaced by SI units.

Unsaturated. Denoting a compound having double or triple bonds in its molecules. Unsaturated compounds can undergo addition reactions as well as substitution.

Uracil. A pyrimidine derivative and one of the major component bases of nucleotides and the nucleic acid RNA.

Urea. The water soluble nitrogenous waste product of mammals and some other vertebrates that is formed by a combination of carbon dioxide and ammonia. Urea also has the distinction of being the first "organic" compound synthesized in the laboratory from inorganic sources.

Urea cycle. The series of biochemical reactions that converts ammonia, which is highly toxic, and carbon dioxide to the much less toxic urea during the excretion of metabolic nitrogen derived from the deamination of excess amino acids. These reactions take place in the liver in mammals and, to a lesser extent, in some other animals. The urea is ultimately excreted in solution in urine.

Ureotelic. Describing animals that excrete nitrogenous waste in the form of urea. Most terrestrial vertebrates are ureotelic, converting ammonium ions formed during the breakdown of amino acids into urea.

Ureter. The duct that carries nitrogenous waste from the kidney to the bladder.

Urethra. The duct that carries nitrogenous waste from the bladder to the outside.

Uric acid. A white, insoluble nitrogenous compound used to store or eliminate nitrogenous waste in birds and other egg laying organisms.

Uricotelic. A nucleoside consisting of one uracil molecule linked to a Dribose sugar molecule. The derived nucleotide uridine diphosphate (UDP) is important in carbohydrate metabolism.

Urinary system. The collection of organs and tissues that perform osmoregulation and excretion. The mammalian urinary system consists of two kidneys each linked to the bladder by a ureter.

Utriculus. A chamber of the inner ear from which the semicircular canals arise. It bears patches of sensory epithelium concerned with detecting changes in the direction and speed of movement.

V

Vaccination. The introduction of antigens into the body to induce production of specific antibodies, either to confer immunity against subsequent infection by the same antigen or, less commonly, to treat a disease. The various types of antigens used include attenuated or dead microorganisms or harmless microorganisms that are closely related to pathogenic types. They are made into a suspension which is usually injected or ingested.

Vacuole. In cells, a membrane bound organelle for containing material usually water. Important cells a large water filled central vacuole is important in water balance.

Vagina. A distensible muscular duct in most female mammals that extends from the uterus (or uteri), betwee the bladder and rectum, to the exterior. It receives the male penis during mating. A similar structure occurs in some invertebrates. The vagina is usually singular, having formed from the lower part of the Mullerian ducts, which fuse in the embryo.

Vagus nerve. One of the pair of nerves that arises from the medulla oblongata in the vertebrate brain and extends into the body to supply the major internal organs. It is the major nerve of the parasympathetic system, carrying motor nerve fibres to the heart, lungs, stomach, intestine, liver, kidneys, etc. It also contains sensory nerve fibres running from the vascera to the brain.

Variation. The extent to which the characteristics of a species can vary. Variation can be caused by environmental and genetic factors. Environmental variation results in differences in the appearance of individuals of a species because of differences in nutrition, disease, population density, etc. Genetic variation is caused by recombination and occasionally mutation.

Variety. The taxonomic group below the subspecies level. The term is often loosely used to describe breeds of livestock or various cultivated forms of agricultural and horticultural species.

Vascular bundle. A strand of conducting tissue found in vascular plants. In plants showing secondary thickening the vascular bundles contain meristematic cambium tissue between the xylem and phloem, but this is generally lacking in plants without secondary thickening.

Vascular plants. Plants containing differentiated cells forming vascular tissue, which comprises the xylem and phloem. Vascular tissue transports water and nutrients through the plant and also provides strength and support. It is characteristic of the tracheophytes. Vascular plants are able to achieve considerable vertical growth upwards and into the soil. They have thus been able to colonize the drier habitats that are inaccessible to the more primitive nonvascular bryophytes.

Vascular tissue. In plants, one of the three main types of tissue, this tissue consists of tubes and associated cells which transport water and nutrients throughout the plant.

Vesicle. Literally "small vessel". A small membrane bound sac for transport of material throughout the cell.

Vas deferens. One of the main pair of ducts in animals that convey sperm from the testis to the exterior. In male mammals, it leads from the epididymis and opens into the urethra just after it leaves the bladder.

Vegetal pole. The end of a spherical animal egg that is opposite the animal pole. The vegetal pole contains most of the yolk and is furthest from the nucleus.

Vegetative. Describing or relating to an involuntary function, such as digestion or the autonomic nervous activity, or to a structure or stage in developmet that is concerned with nutrition and growth rather than with sexual reproduction. Vegetative reproduction is asexual reproduction.

Velamen. A layer surrounding the aerial roots of epiphytic plants which, due to the spongy nature of the cells, is able to soak up surface water. It is made up several layers of dead empty cells situated external to an exodermis. The cells are spirally thickened, and are translucent to allow light through to the photosynthetic tissue beneath.

Veliger. The second larval stage of aquatic mollusks, which develops from the trochophore. During this stage the shell and foot develop and the viscera become rotated so as to produce the asymmetry characteristic of the adult mollusk.

Venter. The swollen base of an archegonium that contains the egg cell (oosphere).

Ventral aorta. The blood vessel in fish and embryo tetrapods that carries deoxygenated blood from the anterior end of the heart and divides to form the six paired aortic arches. In adult tetrapods it is equivalent to the ascending limb of the aorta.

Venule. A small vein that collects deoxygenatedblood from the capillary networks in tissues.

Vermiculite. A very light mica-based substance used as a support material for plant growth in some experiments where soil would be unsuitable. It can, for instance, be sterilized and mineral solutions of known composition can be fed to the plants.

Vernation. The arrangemet of leaves in relation to each other in the bud.

Versatile. Describing an anther that is attached dorsally to the tip of of the filament. This allows the anther to turn freely in the wind, thus aiding pollen dispersal.

Verticillaster. A type of inflorescence in which two oppositely placed cymes are inserted either side of a stem giving the impression of a whorl. This flower structure is typical of the deadnettle family.

Vesicle. A small vacuole of variable origin, such as a Golgi vesicle or pinocytotic vesicle.

Vessel. An advanced form of xylem conducting tissue composed of vertically arranged vessel elements. Vessels are only found in the agiosperms and the gymnosperm order Gnerales.

Vessel element. One of the cells that makes up a xylem vessel. In contrast to tracheids, the most advanced vessel elements are often more broad than long and have horizontal rather than slanting perforation plates.

Violaxanthin. A xanthphyll pigment foundin the brown algae.

Virion. The extracellular inert phase of a virus. A virion consistsof a protein coat surrounding one ormore strands of DNA or RNA. Virions may be polyhedral or helicaland vary greatly in size.

Viroid. A tiny infectious agent found in plants that is similar to a virus but lacks a capsid, consisting simply of a circle of RNA, 300-400 nucleotides long. Viroids replicate within the plant cell and cause characteristic disease symptoms; examples are the potato spindle tuber viroid and the hop stunt viroid.

Virulence. The relative pathogenicity of an organism. Virulence depends on the invasiveness and toxicity of the pathogen. Virulence may very between strain of the same organism.

Virulent phage. A bacteriophage that infects a bacterial cell ad immediately replicates, causing lysis of the host cell.

Vital stains. Nontoxic coloring materials than can be used in dilute concentrations to stain living material without damaging it. Examples of vital stains include Janus green, which selectively stains mitochondria and nerve cells, and trypan blue, which has an affinity for the macrophages of the reticuloendothelial system.

Vitamin. An organic molecule that cannot be produced by the body but is needed by the body in trace amounts. Vitamins come in two general types. The water soluble vitamins such as ascorbic acid(vitamin C) are often important coenzymes or components thereof. The lipid soluble vitamins have a broader range of functions.

Vitreous humor. The firm semifluid jelly that fills the space in the vertebrate eye behind the lens. It contains a delicate network of fibres resembling collagen and helps to maintain the shape of the eyeball.

Vocal cords. A pair of mucous membrane folds stretched across the anterior opening of the larynx. Vibration of the cords by expelled air produces vocal sounds. The pitch of the sound varies according to the length and tension of the cords, which is controlled by muscles of the larynx.

Volkmann's canals. Vascular channels found in bone material. They contain blood vessels that connect with those of the Haversian canals.

W

Wallace's Line. Boundary drawn across the Malay Archipelago, separating Arctogea and Notogea (formerly between Australian and Oriental ZOOGEOGRAPHICAL REGIONS). Not a precise demarcation line, lying along the edge of the south-east Asian continental shelf, between Bali and Lombok, Borneo and Celebes, the Philippines and the Sangai and Talaud Islands. Named by T.H.Huxley after the zoogeographical work of WALLACE.

Wall pressure (Bot). Pressure exerted against the protoplast by plant cell wall; opposed to turgor pressure.

Water vascular system. System of waterfilled canals forming tubular component of echinoderm coelom, usually with direct connection with the exterior. A circumoesophageal water ring internal to the skeleton usually gives off radial water canals which pass through pores in the skeleton wherever tube-feet protrude. Each tube-foot is expanded by a musclar ampulla internal to the skeleton and is coordinated with other in feeding and locomotion.

Wavelength. For light or sound, or other wave, the distance between one crest of the wave to the next crest. For visible light the wavelength is typically measured in nanometers(1 billionth of a meter). For longer wavelengths of light such as radio waves the wavelengths are measured in meters or longer.

Wax. A lipid consisting of long chain fatty acids. Waxes are used by organisms to form water proof layers or structures.

W-chromosome. An alternative notation for the Y-chromosome in organisms where the heterogametic sex is female.

Weismann, August. Theoretical biologist one of the first to appreciate that chromosomes are the physical bearers of hereditary determinants and to forge a comprehensive theory of heredity. With Wilhelm Roux, he advocated the theory of MOSAIC DEVELOPMENT, Best remembered for his theory of the continuity of GERM PLASM. Prolific coiner of terms and entities.

Wernicke's area. Region of the human temporal cortex concerned with the analysis of incoming sounds and located in the dominant hemisphere. Projections lead from Wernicke's area to BROCA'S AREA.

Western blotting. Similar procedure to NORTHERN BLOTTING, but for separating proteins rather than mRNAs.

White matter. Myelinated nerves forming through-conduction pathways of vertebrate BRAIN and SPINAL CORD, with associated glia and blood vessels.

Whorl. Three or more leaves, flowers, sporangia or other plat parts at one point on an axis or node.

Wilting. Condition of plants in which cells lose turgidity and leaves, young stems, etc. droop. Results from excess of transpiratory water loss over absorption. Excessive wilting may be stressful, even irreversible.

Wishbone (furcula). Fused clavicles and interclavicles, diagnostic of birds. Present in ARCHAEOPTERYX.

X

Xanthophyll. A member of a class of oxygen-containing carotenoid pigments, which provide the characteristic yellow and known colours of autumn leaves.

Xenobiotic. Any substance foreign to living systems. Xenobiotics include drugs, pesticides, and carcinogens. Detoxification of such substances occurs mainly in the liver.

Xeric. Denoting conditions characterized by an inadequate supply of water. Xeric conditions exist in arid habitats, externely cold habitats, and in salt marshes. Certain plants are adapted to live in such conditions.

Xeromorphic. Describing the structural modifications of certain plants that enable them to reduce water loss, particularly from their leaves and stems.

X linked gene. A gene located on the X chromosome. See **sex linkage**.

X-rays. Electromagnetic radiation of shorter wavelength than ultraviolet radiation and longer wavelength than gamma radiation.

Xylem. In vascular plants, the Vascular tissue that conducts water and minerals from the roots to the leaves.

Y

Y chromosome. The smaller of the two types of sex chromosome in mammals and certain other animals. It is found only in the heterogametic sex.

Yeasts. A group of unicellular fungi within the class Hemiascomycetae of the phylum Ascomycota. They occur as single cells or as groups or chains of cells; yeasts reproduce asexually by budding and sexually by producing ascopores. Yeasts of the genus Sacharomyces ferment sugars and are used in the baking and brewing industries.

Yeast two-hybrid screen. A technique for detecting an interaction between two proteins by means of expression of a reporter gene in yeast cells. It can be used in high-throughput screening of libraries of genes or potential genes from any species to identify pairs of genes that encode interacting proteins. Essentially, a plasmid carrying a gene for the query protein, termed the 'bait', is introduced to numerous yeast cells, each of which contains a plasmid carrying a particular gene from the gene library, termed the 'fish'. The plasmids are constructed such that both the bair and the fish proteins are expressed in the cells as hybrid proteins, in which the bait or fish protein is fused to a second protein involved in activating expression of a reporter gene. Binding of the bair and fish proteins inside the yeast nucleus allows activation of the reporter gene, and the yeast colony containing those particular genes can be pinpointed and analysed further.

Yolk. The food stored in an egg for the use of the embryo. It can consist mainly of protein or of phospholipids and fats. The eggs of oviparous animals contain a relatively large yolk.

Yolk sac. One of the protective membranes surrounding the embryos of birds, reptiles, and mammals. The embryo derives ourishment from the yolk sac via a system of blood vessels. In birds and reptiles the yolk sac encloses the yolk, in most mammals a fluid replaces the yolk.

Y organ. Either of a pair of glands in the head of certain crustaceans that secrete the hormone ecdysone and play a role in the moulting process.

Z

Zeatin. A naturally occurring cytokinin that was first identified in 1963 in the grains of the maize plant.

Zinc. Symbol Zn. A blue-white metallic element that is a trace element required by living organisms. It functions as the prosthetic group of a number of enzymes.

Zona pellucida. The thick clear membrane surrounding the mammalian egg. It is surrounded by cumulus cells in the freshly ovulated egg, but these disperse as the sperms pass between them and penetrate the zona by enzyme action.

Zoomastigina. A phylum of heterotrophic protoctists, that possess one or more undulipodia for locomotion. It includes both free-living forms and parasites, and aerobic and anaerobic forms. In some recent classifications this phylum has been disbanded and its members dispersed to other taxa according to whether or not they posses mitochondria.

Zooid. An individual member of a colony of invertebrate animals, especially an individual of the phylum Bryozoa.

Zoology. The scientific study of animals, including their anatomy, physiology, biochemistry, genetics, ecology, evolution, and behaviour.

Zoosporangium. A sporangium that produces zoospores, as in some phycomycetes, and green and brown algae.

Zoospore. An asexual motile spore produced by a zoosporangium. It has one or more flagella. These motile spores may encyst in adverse conditions, or may be the means by which the fungus penetrates a new host.

Zxitterion. An ion with both a positive and a negative charge.

Zygomycota. A phylum of saprotrophic or parasitic fungi that includes the bread mould. Their hyphae lack cross walls and they can reproduce asexually by sporangiospores formed within a sporangium or sexually by means of zygospores.

Zygospore. A resistant sexual spore formed when a zygote develops a thick wall. Zygospores are characteristic of the Mucorales and the Conjugales.

Zygote. A diploid cell formed by the union of two gametes. Zygotes give rise to new multicellular organisms.

Zygotene. In meiosis, the stage in midprophase I that is characterized by the active and specific pairig of homologous chromosomes leading to the formation of a haploid number of bivalents.

Zymase. An extract of brewer's yeast containing a mixture of glycolytic enzymes that can perform fermentation.

Zymogen granule. A secretory granule found in large numbers in enzyme-secreting cells. The granules are vesicles containing an inactive precursor of the enzyme, the zygomen, e.g. trypsinogen in exocrine cells of the pancreas. It is activated after secretion via exocytosis at the plasma membrane. The vesicles are usually derived from the Golgi apparatus, where the enzyme is processed and concentrated after synthesis on the rough endoplasmic reticulum.

OOO